Daniel's Prophesy

Daniel's Prophesy

✦

A History of the Future and Message to the Elect

Tom Butler

Dawna Butler

iUniverse, Inc.
New York Bloomington Shanghai

Daniel's Prophesy
A History of the Future and Message to the Elect

iUniverse books may be ordered through booksellers or by contacting:

iUniverse
1663 Liberty Drive
Bloomington, IN 47403
www.iuniverse.com
1-800-Authors (1-800-288-4677)

Because of the dynamic nature of the Internet, any Web addresses or links contained in this book may have changed since publication and may no longer be valid.

The views expressed in this work are solely those of the author and do not necessarily reflect the views of the publisher, and the publisher hereby disclaims any responsibility for them.

Scriptures taken from the HOLY BIBLE, NEW INTERNATIONAL VERSION ®. Copyright © 1973, 1978, 1984 by International Bible Society. Used by permission of Zondervan. All rights reserved.

ISBN: 978-0-595-48595-6 (pbk)
ISBN: 978-0-595-60688-7 (ebk)

Printed in the United States of America

Contents

Introduction

When people hear about the biblical book of Daniel, they usually think of the famous stories read to children such as Daniel in the lions' den and Shadrach, Meshach, and Abednego being rescued from the burning furnace. These stories describe biblical heroes who obeyed God instead of powerful men and the miraculous ways God chose to save his servants. The book of Daniel, however, has so much more to offer than just inspiring heroic stories. Daniel, the author of the book, goes from being a minor member of the royal family in Israel to being one of the top advisors in the world-ruling Gentile empires of Babylon and Persia. And more than just a high-level Jewish advisor to Gentile kings, Daniel became a "highly esteemed" prophet chosen by God to reveal international events that would take place from his time (circa 550 BC) into the distant future. But it's important to remember the greater message of the book of Daniel, as with the writings of all of God's prophets, is true worship of the true God—believing He is who He says He is and obeying what He says to do no matter how difficult.

Because of Daniel's faithfulness in worshiping God, God blessed him with the ability to understand visions and dreams, and through these dreams, God revealed the events of major nations and governments from the time God scattered His nation, ancient Israel, until the time Jesus Christ returns to set up the kingdom of God. There are events and concepts revealed in the book of Daniel that occur nowhere else in the Bible. For example, Daniel is the only book that pinpoints the exact beginning of Jesus Christ's ministry and His death. Daniel is the first to explain how "the Anointed One" would replace the system of animal sacrifices. And the book of Daniel is the only place that reveals the world powers from the time of Daniel until the return of Jesus Christ. The book even includes a discussion of a resurrection to everlasting life. For such a short book, the twelve chapters of Daniel are replete with incredible revelations. The only other book in the Bible similar to Daniel is the New Testament book of Revelation, but even that book doesn't identify future governments the way Daniel does. The book of Daniel outlines awesome future events and the configuration of the nations from his time right up to the return of Jesus Christ, all through the light of worshiping God. It is our hope this book will give insight into the real purpose of the book of Daniel—the importance of worshiping the true God.

"But you, Daniel, close up and seal the words of the scroll until the time of the end."
Daniel 12:4

Preface

The term "kingdom" is not often used in the Western world, but it is used extensively throughout the book of Daniel and the rest of the Bible; God, in fact, is going to set up His own kingdom, so it is an important word to understand when reading the Bible. The book of Daniel describes events through the perspective of kingdoms, and that scriptural view of kingdoms is different from how many of us see the alignment of territories in the geopolitical world today.

The term "kingdom" can refer to a single nation with a monarchy, or it can refer to a group of nations bound together by something they have in common—a ruler, a belief, even proximity. We are familiar with Northern Ireland, Wales, Scotland, and England being referred to as the United Kingdom. We're also familiar with the British Isles, Canada, Australia, New Zealand, and other countries as the British Commonwealth, or Empire. We could also just as easily refer to them as a kingdom.

Have you ever thought of Europe, North America, and South America as a kingdom—a group we could call the Christian Kingdom since all of these countries are Christian, and many of them look to Rome for their religious guidance? In this case, their connection to each other is their religious roots, not governmental structure. People living in these countries may not identify themselves in such fashion, but people from outside these countries would have an easier time categorizing them in this way. To prove this point, I don't think most people in the Western world have a hard time viewing Iran, Turkey, Syria, Egypt, Saudi Arabia, Iraq, and Afghanistan as being part of what we could call the Islamic kingdom. (They were once called the Ottoman Empire, or we could say the Ottoman Kingdom.) Because we live outside of that kingdom, we easily group these Muslim countries together—they're all Islamic—whereas they might not view themselves as a group, instead focusing on their differences such as Sunni versus Shiia, etc. Viewing the Western world as the Christian kingdom might change our perspective on some major historical events. For example, World Wars I and II in Europe go from being seen as worldwide conflicts to something more like civil wars within the Christian kingdom and the West's invasion of Iraq and Afghanistan as the Christian kingdom involving itself in the Islamic kingdom. This view is certainly different than what is found in most history books, but it might be a more accurate view from a biblical perspective.

We also need to be free from our own nationalistic vision and expectations as we read the Bible. It isn't easy to let go of our patriotic view as we read how God views all of mankind and the kingdoms he has allowed to hold power. Many people believe God is on their country's side and that it is unpatriotic to think otherwise. But we need to remember that to understand the Bible we have to align our thinking with God's view, and that might be something a little different than we are used to.

1

Israel

I* remember during a Bible study, I once pointed out to an elderly woman, who had studied the Bible her whole life, that Abraham was not Jewish. She was in disbelief and turned to the pastor in hopes that I was wrong. He reluctantly agreed that "technically" I was correct. It was my turn to be shocked! I couldn't believe a pastor of a mainstream church who had attended a world-famous seminary would be reluctant to reveal what was true and accurate: Abraham was a Hebrew (son of Eber), but not a Jew. The Jewish people came from Judah, Abraham's great-grandson. This same pastor once asked me, "What's this thing you have about Israel?" I relay this story because I believe it highlights the huge disconnect that exists between mainstream Christianity, the new covenant, and ancient Israel. Israel and what it represented is a main focus of God. Jesus, in Matthew 10:6, told His disciples to preach to "the lost sheep of Israel," and in Acts 1, the disciples asked Jesus, "'Lord, are you at this time going to restore the kingdom to Israel?" *"I" refers to Tom Butler.*

He said to them, "It is not for you to know the times or dates the Father has set by his own authority.'" So Israel was an important issue with God even then, and the future "kingdom of God" will be the fulfillment of that promise made to Abraham about his descendants: the nation of Israel.

It is our belief that to understand prophecy you first have to understand God's relationship with ancient Israel: how it came about, why it existed, and what it will be. Almost all prophecy is in one way or another connected to what the Bible calls "the children of Israel." In fact, essentially the whole Bible, with the exception of the first twelve chapters of Genesis, is about Abraham and the nation of Israel. You might ask: "What about Paul and his writings to the Gentiles? That isn't about Israel, is it?" Yes, it is. God through Paul is inviting the Gentiles to share in the promises made to the Israelites (see Romans 11). So we have included this chapter on Israel to give greater understanding on the importance of Israel and its relationship with God, because you cannot navigate the Bible without understanding who, and what, Israel is.

The beginning of the nation of Israel is found in Genesis Chapter 12. God said to Abram, whom he later renamed Abraham:

> I will make you into a great nation and I will bless you; I will make your name great, and you will be a blessing. I will bless those who bless you, and whoever curses you I will curse; and all peoples on earth will be blessed through you. (Genesis 12:2, 3)

God told Abraham more about what would happen to his descendents in Chapter 15:

> Then the Lord said to [Abram], "Know for certain that your descendants will be strangers in a country not their own, and they will be enslaved and mistreated four hundred years. But I will punish the nation they serve as slaves, and afterward they will come out with great possessions. You, however, will go to your fathers in peace and be buried at a good old age. In the fourth generation your descendants will come back here ..." (Genesis 15:13–16)

God gave Abram the name Abraham meaning "father of many." In Genesis Chapter 17, God again spoke to Abraham:

> When Abram was ninety-nine years old, the Lord appeared to him and said, "I am God Almighty; walk before me and be blameless. I will confirm my covenant between me and you and will greatly increase your numbers." Abram fell facedown, and God said to him, "As for me, this is my covenant with you: You will be the father of many nations. No longer will you be called Abram; your name will be Abraham, for I have made you a father of many nations. I will make you very fruitful; I will make nations of you, and kings will come from you. I will establish my covenant as an everlasting covenant between me and you and your descendants after you for the generations to come, to be your God and the God of your descendants after you. The whole land of Canaan, where you are now an alien, I will give as an everlasting possession to you and your descendants after you; and I will be their God. (Genesis 17:1–8)

In this same chapter, God told Abraham he would have a son with his wife, Sarah, and that the covenant between God and Abraham would also be with Isaac, not Ishmael, the son Abraham had through Sarah's servant Hagar.

God also said to Abraham, "As for Sarai your wife, you are no longer to call her Sarai; her name will be Sarah. I will bless her and will surely give you a son by her. I will bless her so that she will be the mother of nations; kings of peoples will come from her."

Abraham fell facedown; he laughed and said to himself, "Will a son be born to a man a hundred years old? Will Sarah bear a child at the age of ninety?" And Abraham said to God, "If only Ishmael might live under your blessing!"

Then God said, "Yes, but your wife Sarah will bear you a son, and you will call him Isaac. I will establish my covenant with him as an everlasting covenant for his descendants after him. (Genesis 17:15–19)

When Abraham was one hundred years old, Sarah gave birth to a son, Isaac, just as God had promised. However, some years later, God made an extremely difficult request in order to test Abraham's faith. God asked Abraham to go to the region of Moriah and sacrifice his only son as a burnt offering. Abraham obeyed God. Just when Abraham was about to kill Isaac, an angel sent by God told Abraham to stop and then provided a ram for the sacrifice instead of Isaac. Because Abraham obeyed God by preparing to sacrifice his son Isaac, God reaffirmed the covenant, but this time, God swore by Himself. As Hebrews 6:13 says: "When God made his promise to Abraham, since there was no one greater for him to swear by, he swore by himself ..."

The angel of the Lord called to Abraham from heaven a second time and said, "I swear by myself, declares the Lord, that because you have done this and have not withheld your son, your only son, I will surely bless you and make your descendants as numerous as the stars in the sky and as the sand on the seashore. Your descendants will take possession of the cities of their enemies, and through your offspring [seed] all nations on earth will be blessed, because you have obeyed me." (Genesis 22:15–18)

God swore by Himself this great promise would be fulfilled. The rest of what is written in the Bible is about Israel, and especially from the time of Jesus forward, it explains how all nations are going to be blessed.

Matthew, the first book of the New Testament, gives Jesus Christ's genealogy starting with Abraham. The apostle Paul tells us: "The promises were spoken to Abraham and to his seed. The Scripture does not say 'and to seeds,' meaning many people, but 'and to your seed,' meaning one person, who is Christ. What I mean is this: The law, introduced 430 years later, does not set aside the covenant previously established by God and thus do away with the promise" (Galatians 3:16, 17).

The author of the book of Hebrews also shows how this promise is being fulfilled:

> When God made his promise to Abraham, since there was no one greater for him to swear by, he swore by himself, saying, "I will surely bless you and give you many descendants." And so after waiting patiently, Abraham received what was promised. Men swear by someone greater than themselves, and the oath confirms what is said and puts an end to all argument. Because God wanted to make the unchanging nature of his purpose very clear to the heirs of what was promised, he confirmed it with an oath. God did this so that, by two unchangeable things in which it is impossible for God to lie, we who have fled to take hold of the hope offered to us may be greatly encouraged. We have this hope as an anchor for the soul, firm and secure. It enters the inner sanctuary behind the curtain, where Jesus, who went before us, has entered on our behalf. He has become a high priest forever, in the order of Melchizedek. (Hebrews 6:13–20)

So, as promised, Abraham had a son whom he named Isaac. Isaac married a woman from his mother's family named Rebekah.

This is the account of Abraham's son Isaac.

> Abraham became the father of Isaac, and Isaac was forty years old when he married Rebekah daughter of Bethuel the Aramean from Paddan Aram and sister of Laban the Aramean.
>
> Isaac prayed to the Lord on behalf of his wife, because she was barren. The Lord answered his prayer, and his wife Rebekah became pregnant. The babies jostled each other within her, and she said, "Why is this happening to me?" So she went to inquire of the Lord. The Lord said to her, "Two nations are in your womb, and two peoples from within you will be separated; one people will be stronger than the other, and the older will serve the younger." (Genesis 25:19–23)

The sons were named Esau and Jacob. The covenant between God and Abraham was established with Isaac; it was now to be carried on through Jacob.

> Jacob left Beersheba and set out for Haran. When he reached a certain place, he stopped for the night because the sun had set. Taking one of the stones there, he put it under his head and lay down to sleep. He had a dream in

which he saw a stairway resting on the earth, with its top reaching to heaven, and the angels of God were ascending and descending on it. There above it stood the Lord, and he said: "I am the Lord, the God of your father Abraham and the God of Isaac. I will give you and your descendants the land on which you are lying. Your descendants will be like the dust of the earth, and you will spread out to the west and to the east, to the north and to the south. All peoples on earth will be blessed through you and your offspring. I am with you and will watch over you wherever you go, and I will bring you back to this land. I will not leave you until I have done what I have promised you. (Genesis 28:10–15)

Abraham, Isaac, and Jacob are called the patriarchs. God later changed Jacob's name to "Israel" (Genesis 32:27, 28 and 35:9, 10). Israel had twelve sons through two wives and their two servants: Reuben, Simeon, Levi, Judah, Issachar, Zebulun, Joseph, Benjamin, Dan, Naphtali, Gad, and Asher (Genesis 35:23–26). He also had a daughter named Dinah (Genesis 30:19–21). As the families increased in size, they were collectively referred to as Israelites. In the book of Exodus, it says, "Now Joseph and all his brothers and all that generation died, but the Israelites were fruitful and multiplied greatly and became exceedingly numerous, so that the land was filled with them" (Exodus 1:6, 7). It is important when reading the Bible to understand God makes a distinction within the whole group: Israelites are known by the house or tribe from which they are descended. Many mistakenly think Israel and Judah are one and the same, but they are not! Many famous Israelites in the Bible came from the tribe of Judah, the greatest being Jesus Christ. But Judah is only one-twelfth of Israel. Moses was from the tribe of Levi (Exodus 2:1–10) as was his brother, Aaron, and John the Baptist (Luke 1:5–13). King Saul, the first king of Israel, and the apostle Paul were both from the tribe of Benjamin (I Samuel 9:1, 2, 15–17). Gideon, in the book of Judges, was from Manasseh (Judges 6:15), and Samson was from Dan (Judges 13:2, 3, 24). God is careful to make these distinctions from within Israel, so it is worthwhile for us to read the Bible with this in mind.

On Passover day, 430 years to the day God made His covenant with Abraham, the Israelites left Egypt in one of the most famous events recorded in the Bible. God led the Israelites out to Mt. Sinai where He asked them to enter into a covenant with Him. God told the Israelites that if they would follow the law He had given them, He would bless them abundantly; however, if they turned away from the law, He would punish and ultimately destroy them by plagues and foreign captivity. All of this is covered in Deuteronomy 28, the blessings and curses chapter. Israel agreed to enter into a covenant with God (Deuteronomy 29:12–

15) around 1450 BC.[1] God expected the Levites to handle the priestly duties in the tabernacle and eventually the temple, but God also promised to give Israel the office of prophet. God told Moses:

> The nations you will dispossess listen to those who practice sorcery or divination. But as for you, the Lord your God has not permitted you to do so. The Lord your God will raise up for you a prophet like me from among your own brothers. You must listen to him. For this is what you asked of the Lord your God at Horeb on the day of the assembly when you said, "Let us not hear the voice of the Lord our God nor see this great fire anymore, or we will die."
>
> The Lord said to me: "What they say is good. I will raise up for them a prophet like you from among their brothers; I will put my words in his mouth, and he will tell them everything I command him. If anyone does not listen to my words that the prophet speaks in my name, I myself will call him to account. But a prophet who presumes to speak in my name anything I have not commanded him to say, or a prophet who speaks in the name of other gods, must be put to death. (Deuteronomy 18:14–22)

The prophet told the nation of Israel what was on God's mind: warning the people when they were disobeying God, letting them know whether God would bless them in battle, or any other important information that impacted the nation. The office of prophet is important because it is from this promise we have the subject of our book, Daniel. He and many other famous men such as Elijah, Elisha, Isaiah, Jeremiah, and Ezekiel told the people of Israel what God wanted them to know.

Over the next two hundred years or so, God settled Israel into Canaan, and from about 1200 to 938 BC, under Kings Saul, David, and Solomon, Israel became a powerful and prosperous world-ruling nation. For the most part, Israel did not follow the laws God had given them, and from time to time, Israel strayed so much that God sent a prophet to warn the nation of punishment. Usually, the nation of Israel repented, but only after God inflicted some form of punishment on them. In 938 BC, Israel split into two nations (see 2 Chronicles from 9:30 on): The northern tribes kept the name Israel, and the southern tribes of Judah, Benjamin, and some Levites became the nation of Judah.

The greatest sin Israel or Judah could commit was the sin of idolatry—the worship of other gods. This act made God angry, and it was this sin that made the prophets warn the people to repent or face the wrath of God. Nowhere is this better illustrated than in the book of the prophet Hosea. Hosea was told to marry a prostitute who continued to have many adulterous affairs. Over and over, God told Hosea to take her back because God said that was what it was like being married to Israel. When the prophets warned the nation they were disobeying God, the people ignored, ridiculed, or killed them. In 722 BC, the nation of Assyria conquered and destroyed the northern tribes of Israel, as God had warned would happen through the prophets. God also wiped out the identity of these tribes by dispersing them among the conquering nations and causing them to forget their ancestry. To this day, there is no knowledge of people from the houses of Reuben, Gad, Asher, Naphtali, Joseph (Ephraim and Manasseh), Dan, Simeon, Issachar, and Zebulun. God followed through on his promise made at Sinai to bring destruction on the nation of Israel if they were disobedient and worshiped other gods, breaking the covenant they had made with God.

After 722 BC, only the nation of Judah, with some Benjaminites and Levites, remained from the once-powerful nation of Israel. After Israel was taken into captivity, the nation of Judah was small and surrounded by enemies, but God promised to protect her if she was willing to follow the covenant made at Sinai. For a while, Judah was compliant, but soon, she too began to be unfaithful to God. God sent the prophet Isaiah to warn the people of Judah that unless they changed their ways, they too would be destroyed. God sent other prophets such as Ezekiel and Jeremiah to warn and encourage the people to turn from their evil and remember the covenant they made with Him.

All of this brings us to 605 BC, when the prophet Jeremiah prophesied against the people of Judah, who at this time had to pay heavy tribute to Egypt, that the house of the Lord on Mount Moriah in Jerusalem would be deserted and the people would have trouble.

> Early in the reign of Jehoiakim son of Josiah king of Judah, this word came from the Lord: "This is what the Lord says: Stand in the courtyard of the Lord's house and speak to all the people of the towns of Judah who come to worship in the house of the Lord. Tell them everything I command you; do not omit a word. Perhaps they will listen and turn from his evil way. Then I will relent and not bring on them the disaster I was planning because of the evil they have done. Say to them, 'This is what the Lord says: If you do not listen to me and follow my law, which I have set before you, and if you do not listen to the words of my servants the prophets, whom I have sent to you again and again (though you have not listened), then I will make this house like Shiloh and this city an object of cursing among all the nations of the earth.'"
> (Jeremiah 26:1–6)

Unfortunately, the king and the people did not turn from worshiping other gods, so the king tore up and burned Jeremiah's prophecy to the nation of Judah; Jahoiakim also put the prophet Uriah to death for prophesying the same message

Jeremiah did. Later, in 605 BC, "Jahoiakim was confronted with a Babylonian invasion. In the decisive battle at Carchemish in early summer, the Egyptians were routed by the Babylonians. By August, Nebuchadrezzar had advanced far enough into southern Palestine to claim treasure and hostages in Jerusalem—Daniel and his friends being the most noteworthy among the Judean captives."[2]

Eventually, Judah would live between Egyptian vassalage and the threat of Babylonian conquest as a result of the people's failure to repent and turn back to God, instead continuing in the worship of idols and false gods. Finally, in 586 BC, Jerusalem, under King Zedekiah, fell to King Nebuchadnezzar of Babylon and everything in the city and countryside was totally destroyed. All of this history can be reviewed in more depth in the biblical books of First and Second Kings and First and Second Chronicles. In all, Judah lasted about two hundred years longer than Israel. The difference between the two is that God did not eviscerate the identity of the Jewish people.

Now we have arrived at the point in history where we can pick up with the events of the book of Daniel. God had brought about the defeat of Judah, including the city of Jerusalem, and Daniel had been carried off to Babylon with some other members of the royal family. It would seem that God's dealings with Israel were over, except that He made a promise to Abraham and swore by Himself it would be accomplished. So now, because of God's unfailing promise, comes the rest of the story of … Israel.

2

Element Man

✦

Gold, Silver, Bronze, and Iron and Baked Clay

The most powerful ruler on earth was having trouble getting a good night's rest. King Nebuchadnezzar of Babylon was having vivid, troubling dreams that made no sense, so he demanded his spiritual advisors come to him immediately! The advisors knew the routine: the king would relate his dream and they would give him their interpretation. "O king, live forever! Tell your servants the dream, and we will interpret it" (Daniel 2:4).

But tonight was different. Tonight, the king replied: "This is what I have firmly decided: If you do not tell me what my dream was and interpret it, I will have you cut into pieces and your houses turned into piles of rubble. But if you tell me the dream and explain it, you will receive from me gifts and rewards and great honor. So tell me the dream and interpret it for me" (Daniel 2:5, 6).

The spiritual advisors were shocked; their lives were at stake over an impossible request! "There is not a man on earth who can do what the king asks! No king, however great and mighty, has ever asked such a thing of any magician or enchanter or astrologer. What the king asks is too difficult. No one can reveal it to the king except the gods, and they do not live among men" (Daniel 2:10, 11).

The Bible explains the rest of the story: Daniel, under the same death threat, found out what the king was asking and requested more time so he could interpret the dream for him. Daniel and his three friends asked God for mercy concerning this request from the king so they would not be executed. "During the night the mystery was revealed to Daniel in a vision. Then Daniel praised the God of heaven" (Daniel 2:19).

When Daniel was brought before King Nebuchadnezzar, he was asked: "Are you able to tell me what I saw in my dream and interpret it?"

Daniel replied, "No wise man, enchanter, magician, or diviner can explain to the king the mystery he has asked about, but there is a God in heaven who reveals mysteries. He has shown King Nebuchadnezzar what will happen in days to come. Your dream and the visions that passed through your mind as you lay on your bed are these …" (Daniel 2:26–28).

> "As you were lying there, O king, your mind turned to things to come, and the revealer of mysteries showed you what is going to happen. As for me, this mystery has been revealed to me, not because I have greater wisdom than other living men, but so that you, O king, may know the interpretation and that you may understand what went through your mind.
>
> "You looked, O king, and there before you stood a large statue—an enormous, dazzling statue, awesome in appearance. The head of the statue was made of pure gold, its chest and arms of silver, its belly and thighs of bronze, its legs of iron, its feet partly of iron and partly of baked clay. While you were watching, a rock was cut out, but not by human hands. It struck the statue on its feet of iron and clay and smashed them. Then the iron, the clay, the bronze, the silver and the gold were broken to pieces at the same time and became like chaff on a threshing floor in the summer. The wind swept them away without leaving a trace. But the rock that struck the statue became a huge mountain and filled the whole earth.
>
> "This was the dream, and now we will interpret it to the king. You, O King, are the king of kings. The God of heaven has given you dominion and power and might and glory; in your hands he has placed mankind and the beasts of the field and the birds of the air. Wherever they live, he has made you ruler over them all. You are that head of gold.
>
> "After you, another kingdom will rise, inferior to yours. Next, a third kingdom, one of bronze, will rule over the whole earth. Finally, there will be a fourth kingdom, strong as iron—for iron breaks and smashes everything—and as iron breaks things to pieces, so it will crush and break all the others. Just as you saw that the feet and toes were partly of baked clay and partly of iron, so this will be a divided kingdom; yet it will have some of the strength of iron in it, even as you saw iron mixed with clay. As the toes were partly iron and partly clay, so this kingdom will be partly strong and partly brittle. And just as you saw the iron mixed with baked clay, so the people will be a mixture and will not remain united, any more than iron mixes with clay.
>
> "In the time of those kings, the God of heaven will set up a kingdom that will never be destroyed, nor will it be left to another people. It will crush all those kingdoms and bring them to an end, but it will itself endure forever. This is the meaning of the vision of the rock cut out of a mountain, but not by

human hands—a rock that broke the iron, the bronze, the clay, the silver and the gold to pieces.

"The great God has shown the king what will take place in the future. The dream is true and the interpretation is trustworthy."

Then King Nebuchadnezzar fell prostrate before Daniel and paid him honor and ordered that an offering and incense be presented to him. The king said to Daniel, "Surely your God is the God of gods and the Lord of kings and a revealer of mysteries, for you were able to reveal this mystery." (Daniel 2:29–47)

Here is Daniel in the role of prophet, but he wasn't sent to the nation of Israel like most of the prophets before him. Instead, he was sent to a Gentile king with a message that had never been heard before. The message was about the Gentile kingdoms that would rule until God set up His everlasting kingdom.

Who were these kingdoms Nebuchadnezzar dreamed about? We don't have to guess because God, through the Bible, identified three of the four kingdoms. The interpretation of the dream begins in verse 36 where God tells King Nebuchadnezzar, the ruler of the Babylonian Empire, that he is the head of gold and his power to rule comes from God. God had removed His power from Israel since they no longer had God in their midst as their ruler. Daniel 1:2 says: "And the Lord delivered Jehoiakim king of Judah into his [Nebuchadnezzar's] hand, along with some of the articles from the temple of God. These he carried off to the temple of his god in Babylonia and put in the treasure house of his god." God then gave a succession of Gentile kingdoms power to rule.

After the head of gold—the Babylonian Empire—was the chest of silver, a kingdom God said was inferior to Nebuchadnezzar's empire. In Chapter 5 verse 30, there's an event that describes the transfer of power from the head of gold to the chest of silver. "That very night Belshazzar, king of the Babylonians, was slain, and Darius the Mede took over the kingdom, at the age of sixty-two." The Medes, under Darius, succeeded the Babylonian empire. This biblical account is supported by history, showing the Medes ruled from around 539 BC through the next two hundred or so years. During this time, the Medes ascended to become a great empire, ruling from the shores of Europe to the borders of India, with such great kings as Xerxes and Cyrus II.

After the second kingdom came the third kingdom—the belly and thighs of bronze. In Daniel 11:2–3, we see who was prophesied to succeed the Medo/Persian Empire after the time of Xerxes: "Now then, I tell you the truth: Three more kings will appear in Persia, and then a fourth, who will be far richer than all the others. When he has gained power by his wealth, he will stir up everyone against the kingdom of Greece. Then a mighty king will appear, who will rule with great power and do as he pleases." This mighty king was Alexander the Great of Greece who defeated the Persians in 333 BC and conquered almost the entire known European and Middle Eastern world. After he died in 323 BC, the Greek empire was broken up into several smaller kingdoms. "After he has appeared, his empire will be broken up and parceled out toward the four winds of heaven. It will not go to his descendants, nor will it have the power he exercised, because his empire will be uprooted and given to others" (Daniel 2:4). Alexander's Greek empire continued to rule, but in a divided state.

And then came the fourth kingdom. In the statue, this kingdom is described as legs of iron and toes of iron and clay—two materials that don't mix. This kingdom was strong and crushed, broke, and smashed everything, but later on, it was divided—made up of people who did not remain united. We aren't told through Daniel who the fourth kingdom is, which is the last kingdom, the kingdom that will be on earth when God destroys man's kingdoms and sets up His kingdom. The book of Daniel doesn't call this fourth kingdom by name; there is no biblical account of a ruler from someplace conquering the Greek empire. Instead, we need to rely on what we see in history. Because it would seem the Greek empire is no longer a dominant world power, and obviously, God hasn't set up His kingdom yet, we'll see what recorded history has to say.

History records that around 70–80 BC, the Romans conquered the remaining subdivisions of the Greek empire (Ptolemys, Seleucids, et al.). And by 50 BC, under Julius Caesar, Rome became a dominant, world-ruling empire. It was under this kingdom that Jesus Christ lived, taught, and was crucified. At its height, the Roman Empire covered subjugated territory from England to India. The Roman Empire ruled the world from about 50 BC to around AD 550; that's 600 years of dominant involvement in world affairs. It would be hard not to include the Romans as the fourth empire, so therefore, I think it's safe to conclude through historical accounts that the fourth kingdom, the legs of iron and toes of iron and clay, is the Roman Empire. However, if the Roman Empire ends somewhere around 550, and it is the fourth empire of the statue dream, we have a problem with our logic because we still have 1,500 years of history left. It would all have worked out if Jesus Christ had set up His kingdom when the Roman Empire collapsed around 550, but He didn't, so we have to take a closer look at how we describe this fourth kingdom.

There is, in our belief, no question on the first three kingdoms: the Babylonians, Medo/Persians, and the Greeks are the first three parts of the statue. But remember, the fourth part of the statue does have two parts. The legs are of iron and the feet are a mix of iron and baked clay; therefore, it is possible that the fourth kingdom has two variant looks. One part of the empire looks one way, and the other has similarities, but is different looking.

However, before we look beyond 550, there is a rather interesting connection that ties all four empires together at this point. Anyone who researches ancient Middle Eastern religions will ultimately run into the pantheon of gods called the Avesta. Its origins are in Babylon somewhere around 1100 BC; however, it is possible that some of these beliefs may go back as far as ancient Egypt. Within the pantheon, there were many gods, but chief among them were Ahrahu Mazda, the father god; Anahita, the queen of heaven; and her son, Mithra. These were the gods of the Babylonians, and when Babylon fell to the Medes and Persians, they too worshiped Mithra, whose chief prophet was a man known as Zoroaster. When the Greeks conquered the Persians, Mithra worship spread westward back toward the European citadels. Ultimately, the conquering Roman soldiers inculcated Mithra into their religious system, and by AD 250, Mithra was the official religion of the Roman Empire up to, and including, the time of Emperor Constantine. It is Constantine who used his authority around AD 323 to take the ancient pagan festivals and give them Christian meanings after allegedly seeing a cross in the sky. He declared Christianity the official religion of the empire; now, the world-ruling empire of Rome had the banner of Christianity. However, this change from a "pagan" culture to a "Christian" empire was really no change at all, or at the very least, it was a change in name only because the pagan festivals and symbols were maintained but with a Christian appellation. Going forward, the Roman emperors continued to be Pontifix Maximus—both ruler and religious leader—until around the 400s, when the mantle was split in two with the position of emperor held by one man, the position of religious leader held by another. The one common denominator to the parts of the statue in Daniel 2 is that all of the empires worshiped the same god and all of the rulers served as the connection to the gods, or as deities themselves. Once God handed Israel over to the Babylonian king, there was no longer a nation on earth led by God. The statue's gold, silver, bronze, and iron and iron and baked clay apparently are all united by their worship of the ancient Babylonian religious system, of course wrapped in each empire's cultural traditions and names.

So sometime in the mid 300s, the world-ruling Roman Empire became the Christian Roman Empire. However, in the next three hundred years, it began to suffer decline and by AD 550–600, it ultimately fell. Since we believe the Roman Empire is the fourth kingdom, and the vision God revealed to King Nebuchadnezzar only had four kingdoms, where does it leave us with 1,500 years of history still to go? This is where the statue's description "its legs of iron, its feet partly of iron and partly of baked clay" comes in. The statue parts flow seamlessly until the return of Jesus Christ; each part follows the previously mentioned section without gaps in time. Because we're told there are only four kingdoms, we know the feet/toes are part of the legs of iron—the Roman Empire; however, there is something different about them because they have baked clay mixed with the iron. God says this describes a "divided kingdom," a kingdom that is partly strong and partly brittle, people who are a "mixture and will not remain united." So after what historians identify as the fall of the Roman Empire, its successor must somehow have a connection to Rome, or the Roman system. To help identify who, or what, this may be, let's take a look at the countries, or empires, that have been dominant in the world since Rome fell around AD 600.

The area covered by Roman rule in the 600s had been reduced to mainly the Western/European world. We see that around the late eighth century, the Germanic people under Charlemagne, Otto, and Fredrick the Great created what was known to some as the Empire in the West. This empire covered much of central Europe and became known as the Roman Empire and ultimately the Holy Roman Empire because the rulers sought the blessings of popes in Rome for their authority. Although this empire continued in name, its influence waned with the emergence of the Italians during the Renaissance (around 1200). This period began great exploration in art, science, economics, and geography. Later, in the fifteenth century, Spain emerged as a great power. Both Spain and Portugal began to expand their influence to lands outside Europe. World trade and commerce made these Iberian countries so wealthy that by the middle of the sixteenth century, Spain had become the most powerful nation in the world—It was said the sun never set on the Spanish Empire. (This phrase was also later used to describe the British Empire.) Concomitantly, France and England were becoming major players.

By the end of the seventeenth century, the nations of Spain, England, France, Portugal, Holland, and Denmark had expanded their influence to the far-flung regions of the world through the influence of their colonies. During the middle of the eighteenth century, England began to emerge as the number one power, replacing Spain as the dominant European power. Except for a brief period of French expansion during Napoleon's time, England's empire had replaced Spain as the world's greatest empire. But in the early twentieth century, a great war broke out and cost England dearly. As we've seen with previous declines, as one empire falls, another empire rises. By 1920, America began to eclipse England as the world's new super power. Since 1900, the U.S. has grown into the greatest mono-power since Alexander's Greece. At the close of WWII, because of improvements in transportation and communication, America and her European allies formed a strong bond known as the free world/the democracies/the West. Over the next fifty years, together they would battle Communism, tyranny, and terrorism. At this writing, America and her European allies control the economic and military power in the world. According to author Max Boot, who sits on the Council of Foreign Relations, in a speech before the San Diego City Club in November 2006, the Europeans and Americans have grown in power to control "84% of the world's surface." That's a pretty good definition of dominant. So we can say that since AD 600 the world has been under the strong influence of the Western powers of Europe and, more recently, America.

Now that we have identified the major Western powers that followed the collapse of the Roman government in AD 600, we have to ask: What connection do the Western nations—Europe and the Americas—have to ancient Rome that would make them the feet and toes of iron and baked clay? The powerful influence of the Roman Empire no longer exists, but the Roman Christian system of religion continues to exert its power to this very day! The Western nations have one common denominator: their religion is Roman Christian or a derivative of Roman Christianity. The pope still holds the title that many Roman emperors held—Pontifix Maximus. Western countries are either Catholic or Protestant because they "protested" the Catholic religion. Protestants believed there should be significant changes made in the Catholic faith, but the major beliefs of the two religions are the same—Christmas, Easter, the Trinity, the cross, doctrines of heaven and hell, and much more. In fact, all accepted mainstream Christianity is derived from Roman Catholicism. As the Western world/Christian empire colonized and controlled the flow of commerce, it also spread the religion of the empire. When it comes to fulfilling the description of the toes of Daniel 2, there isn't even a close second to the nations of the Western world. These nations are a group of people who are not united, partly strong and partly brittle, "a divided kingdom," but they all have a form of Roman Christianity in common. It may be difficult to see ourselves as part of an empire, or "kingdom," grouped together by religion because we make a great distinction between Catholics and Protestants, Europeans and Americans (North and South America), and we highlight the number of non-Christian people who live among us, even though they make up less than 10 percent of the population. If you don't believe that, just take a look around at Christmastime. But the view is different from outside the Western world, and two recent incidents come to mind as examples. A Turkish official, commenting on the European Economic Community's (European Union) reluctance to admit his Islamic country to the organization, referred to the Western nations as a "Christian club." And, after Pope Benedict XVI offended Muslims by his quote in September 2006, an extremist group in Iraq threatened the people of the Western nations, referring to them as "all worshippers of the cross." Non-Christian nations clearly see the Christian bond of Western nations.

So we now see that the successor governments to the Roman Empire are the Western nations under the banner of Roman Christianity. This block of countries can accurately be called the Roman Christian Empire: They are represented by the feet and toes of iron and baked clay. So with all of this in mind, we think we can conclude that we are currently in the fourth empire as described in Nebuchadnezzar's dream: the feet and toes of iron and baked clay.

Now, before going further, it might be worth going back and taking a closer look at the religion of the Roman Christian Empire. The following information is given with the hope that the reader will do further research—It is only a primer for more research, not an exhaustive study; that would be a book in itself. The purpose here is to give enough information so that the reader can understand the origins of Christianity as they relate to what is written in Daniel and Revelation. We strongly encourage further research, which we believe will only strengthen the information given here. Many Christians already know, and will readily admit, that their religious celebrations all have pagan origins. They know December 25 is the sun god's birthday, not Jesus Christ's, and that events such as Easter, Lent, Palm Sunday, Fat Tuesday, Ash Wednesday, Good Friday, Halloween (also known as the festival of the dead), Advent, New Year's Day (still a holy day in Catholicism), and many other familiar days have their roots in ancient pagan worship. As mentioned previously, when Constantine converted Rome to Christianity, he simply took the old religious festivals and placed Christian labels on them. The new Christian religion of the Roman Empire was really nothing more than the old Babylonian system with a new name. But even though the origins are pagan, Christians reason that their worship is dedicated to Christ and so it's acceptable and pleasing to God because, after all, their hearts are in the right place. But there is a problem with this reasoning: This isn't a conclusion you can reach if you read the Bible. Throughout the Bible, ancient Israel gives God the exact same defense of their own worship system, but God never accepts it. In fact, because the people reject worshiping God the way He prescribes, He allows them to be defeated and taken into captivity. God dictates the way He wants to be worshiped, and inculcating pagan deities into that worship *has never been acceptable!* Reading the first few chapters of the book of Ezekiel gives you an understanding as to how God feels about mixing pagan worship with true worship. In Chapter 8, Ezekiel says:

> ... while I was sitting in my house and the elders of Judah were sitting before me, the hand of the Sovereign Lord came upon me there. I looked, and I saw a figure like that of a man. From what appeared to be his waist down he was like fire, and from there up his appearance was as bright as glowing metal. He stretched out what looked like a hand and took me by the hair of my head. The Spirit lifted me up between earth and heaven and in visions of God he took me to Jerusalem, to the entrance to the north gate of the inner court, where the idol that provokes to jealousy stood. And there before me was the glory of the God of Israel, as in the vision I had seen in the plain.
>
> Then he said to me, "Son of man, look toward the north." So I looked, and in the entrance north of the gate of the altar I saw this idol of jealousy.
>
> And he said to me, "Son of man, do you see what they are doing—the utterly detestable things the house of Israel is doing here, things that will drive me far from my sanctuary? But you will see things that are even more detestable."
>
> Then he brought me to the entrance to the court. I looked, and I saw a hole in the wall. He said to me, "Son of man, now dig into the wall." So I dug into the wall and saw a doorway there.
>
> And he said to me, "Go in and see the wicked and detestable things they are doing here." So I went in and looked, and I saw portrayed all over the walls all kinds of crawling things and detestable animals and all the idols of the house of Israel. In front of them stood seventy elders of the house of Israel, and Jaazaniah son of Shaphan was standing among them. Each had a censer in his hand, and a fragrant cloud of incense was rising.
>
> He said to me, "Son of man, have you seen what the elders of the house of Israel are doing in the darkness, each at the shrine of his own idol? They say, 'The Lord does not see us; the Lord has forsaken the land.'" Again, he said, "You will see them doing things that are even more detestable."
>
> Then he brought me to the entrance to the north gate of the house of the Lord, and I saw women sitting there, mourning for Tammuz. He said to me, "Do you see this, son of man? You will see things that are even more detestable than this."
>
> He then brought me into the inner court of the house of the Lord, and there at the entrance to the temple, between the portico and the latar, were about twenty-five men. With their backs toward the temple of the Lord and their faces toward the east, they were bowing down to the sun in the east.
>
> He said to me, "Have you seen this, son of man? Is it a trivial matter for the house of Judah to do the detestable things they are doing here? Must they also fill the land with violence and continually provoke me to anger? Look at them putting the branch to their nose! Therefore I will deal with them in

anger; I will not look on them with pity or spare them. Although they shout in my ears, I will not listen to them." (Ezekiel 8:1–18)

Because His people were worshiping other gods, this is what the true God did:

"... Go throughout the city of Jerusalem and put a mark on the foreheads of those who grieve and lament over all the detestable things that are done in it."
   As I listened, he said to the others, "Follow him through the city and kill, without showing pity or compassion. Slaughter old men, young men and maidens, women and children, but do not touch anyone who has the mark. Begin at my sanctuary." So they began with the elders who were in front of the temple. (Ezekiel 9:4–6)

In Deuteronomy 28, God says, "If you fully obey the Lord your God and carefully follow all his commands ..." and then He lists the blessings that will be poured out on His people. But in verse 15, He says, "However, if you do not obey the Lord your God and do not carefully follow all his commands ..." and then He lists the curses He will send on His people. One of the curses, in verse 64, is: "Then the Lord will scatter you among all nations, from one end of the earth to the other. There you will worship other gods—gods of wood and stone, which neither you nor your fathers have known." This prophecy in Deuteronomy 28, symbolized by the statue in Daniel 2, is being fulfilled. God has handed His people over to these kingdoms who serve gods of wood and stone, as He promised, starting with captivity in Babylon. In the book of Revelation, at the time of the end, these same gods are still being worshiped. Chapter 17 in the book of Revelation talks about a religious system that manipulates the kings of the earth shortly before the return of Jesus Christ. The name of that system is rather interesting: "MYSTERY BABYLON THE GREAT THE MOTHER OF PROSTITUTES AND THE ABOMINATIONS OF THE EARTH." This religious system, symbolized by the feet and toes of iron and baked clay, is directly linked to the head of gold where it all started—Babylon. It's startling to think that many people worship the same god the way Nebuchadnezzar did 2,500 years ago. This system is still active. However, there will be a time in the future when God ends the practice of worshiping gods of wood and stone and sets up His kingdom. At the time of the end during the fourth kingdom, God says, "In the time of those kings, the God of heaven will set up a kingdom that will never be destroyed, nor will it be left to another people. It will crush all those kingdoms and bring them to an end, but it will itself endure forever. This is the meaning of the rock cut out of the mountain, but not by human hands—a rock that broke the iron, the bronze, the clay, the silver and gold to pieces" (Daniel 2:44, 45).

At this point, it's worth remembering why God revealed these events to Daniel in the first place. Long ago, God had made a covenant with ancient Israel, but they failed to follow the covenant they agreed to keep. The book of Judges relates that:

> The people served the Lord throughout the lifetime of Joshua and of the elders who outlived him and who had seen all the great things the Lord had done for Israel.
>
> After that whole generation had been gathered to their fathers, another generation grew up, who knew neither the Lord nor what he had done for Israel. Then the Israelites did evil in the eyes of the Lord and served the Baals. They forsook the Lord, the God of their fathers, who had brought them out of Egypt. They followed and worshiped various gods of the peoples around them. They provoked the Lord to anger because they forsook him and served Baal and the Ashtoreths. In his anger against Israel the Lord handed them over to raiders who plundered them. He sold them to their enemies all around, whom they were no longer able to resist. Whenever Israel went out to fight, the hand of the Lord was against them to defeat them, just as he had sworn to them. They were in great distress.
>
> Then the Lord raised up judges, who saved them out of the hands of these raiders. Yet they would not listen to their judges but prostituted themselves to other gods and worshiped them. Unlike their fathers, they quickly turned from the way in which their fathers had walked, the way of obedience to the Lord's commands. Whenever the Lord raised up a judge for them, he was with the judge and saved them out of the hands of their enemies as long as the judge lived; for the Lord had compassion on them as they groaned under those who oppressed and afflicted them. But when the judge died, the people returned to ways even more corrupt than those of their fathers, following other gods and serving and worshiping them. They refused to give up their evil practices and stubborn ways. (Judges 2:7, 10–19)

God's number one accusation against ancient Israel throughout the Old Testament is that they stopped worshiping Him and started worshiping other gods. God sent Israel, as He warned He would in Deuteronomy 28, into captivity and gave great power and authority to the Gentile nation of Babylon and the subsequent nations revealed in Nebuchadnezzar's dream. The dream given to King Nebuchadnezzar tells us God is giving the Gentile nations, who worship the gods of wood and stone, authority to rule until Jesus Christ returns to set up His kingdom. God wanted His faithful followers to know He still has a plan for a future kingdom. Element Man, the statue in Nebuchadnezzar's dream, is a description of what will occur after the destruction of the nation of ancient Israel in 586 BC until the return of Jesus Christ. God's destruction of Element Man sets the stage for the creation of a divine kingdom here on earth. It will fulfill the very promise God made to Abraham: that all nations on earth will be blessed through his seed, Jesus Christ. The divine kingdom of God will end man's rule on earth and begin a kingdom of everlasting peace and prosperity, something mankind has never known. This is the end point of Element Man.

God hasn't changed. He still wants His people to worship Him. As we explore the book of Daniel, we see that this book, famous for its prophecies, may not really be about prophecy after all. Prophecy isn't an end in itself, but a means to an end. God uses, or gives, prophecy to reveal Himself and help people worship Him. It's easy to get caught up in the excitement of understanding future events that are foretold in the Bible, but by itself, prophecy really leads to nothing. Knowing the future is of no advantage unless it helps lead you somewhere, and that somewhere should always be to worship the Ancient of Days—the Living God—the God of Abraham, Isaac, and Jacob—the God of Israel. In the end, as we will see, the book of Daniel is not really about prophecy the way many people think it is. The book of Daniel is a book about worship: failure to worship the true God and the curses that result and proper worship of God in the way He desires, and the blessings that come from obedience to God.

3

Another Troubling Dream

We are now going to jump to Daniel Chapter 7. Although it isn't the next chapter chronologically, it covers the four kingdoms from the time of Daniel to the end of the age, just as Chapter 2 did through the vision of Element Man.

Chapter 7 begins with a new Babylonian king. After King Nebuchadnezzar died, his son Belshazzar became king. The chapter starts off in the first year of his reign. The Bible says there was another troubling dream, but this time, it was Daniel, not the king, who had the dream. After the vision, he wrote down the substance of the dream.

> Daniel said: "In my vision at night I looked, and there before me were the four winds of heaven churning up the great sea. Four great beasts, each different from the others, came up out of the sea.
>
> "The first was like a lion, and it had the wings of an eagle. I watched until its wings were torn off and it was lifted from the ground so that it stood on two feet like a man, and the heart of a man was given to it.
>
> "And there before me was a second beast, which looked like a bear. It was raised up on one of its sides, and it had three ribs in its mouth between its teeth. It was told, 'Get up and eat your fill of flesh!'
>
> "After that, I looked, and there before me was another beast, one that looked like a leopard. And on its back it had four wings like those of a bird. This beast had four heads, and it was given authority to rule.
>
> "After that, in my vision at night I looked, and there before me was a fourth beast—terrifying and frightening and very powerful. It had large iron teeth; it crushed and devoured its victims and trampled underfoot whatever was left. It was different from all the former beasts, and it had ten horns.
>
> "While I was thinking about the horns, there before me was another horn, a little one, which came up among them; and three of the first horns were uprooted before it. This horn had eyes like the eyes of a man and a mouth that spoke boastfully." (Daniel 7:2–8)

In verse 9, Daniel says:

"As I looked, thrones were set in place, and the Ancient of Days took his seat. His clothing was white as snow; the hair of his head was white like wool. His throne was flaming with fire, and its wheels were all ablaze. A river of fire was flowing, coming out from before him. Thousands upon thousands attended him; ten thousand times ten thousand stood before him. The court was seated, and the books were opened." (Daniel 7:9, 10)

Daniel then continues the description from verse 8 of a beast with a horn having eyes and a mouth that spoke boastfully:

"Then I continued to watch because of the boastful words the horn was speaking. I kept looking until the beast was slain and its body destroyed and thrown into the blazing fire. (The other beasts had been stripped of their authority, but were allowed to live for a period of time.)
    "In my vision at night I looked, and there before me was one like a son of man, coming with the clouds of heaven. He approached the Ancient of Days and was led into his presence. He was given authority, glory and sovereign power; all peoples, nations and men of every language worshiped him. His dominion is an everlasting dominion that will not pass away, and his kingdom is one that will never be destroyed." (Daniel 7:11–14)

At this point, Daniel was deeply troubled by the vision; he was disturbed by what he saw, so he approached "one of those standing there and asked him the true meaning of all this." The individual standing there was apparently one of those tending to the Ancient of Days because there wasn't anyone else mentioned in the vision up to this point. This being was most likely an angel, perhaps Gabriel the messenger, and Daniel asks him the meaning of the entire vision.

"So he told me and gave me the interpretation of these things: 'The four great beasts are four kingdoms that will rise from the earth. But the saints of the Most High will receive the kingdom and will possess it forever—yes, for ever and ever.'" (Daniel 7:16–18)

Before going any further, it's worth stopping and digesting what is said in verses 17 and 18. Daniel is told the kingdoms of this world will end and the kingdom of the Most High will succeed them. This same kingdom is exactly what Jesus Christ spent most of His ministry talking about. It is easy to let this slip by, but it's no small matter—this is the hope of all the dispossessed Israelites who are in exile in Babylon and the subsequent empires and all people called by God. In the book of Matthew, it says, "From that time on Jesus began to preach, 'Repent, for the kingdom of heaven is near'" (Matthew 4:17). This is the very hope God is revealing to Daniel in this vision.

There is something else that needs to be mentioned here as well. Today, there are many people who believe the kingdom of God is already here, but the book of Daniel totally refutes that belief. No kingdom or nation ruling now remotely represents the kingdom of God talked about in Daniel 7:18, and, as we'll see, the discussion in subsequent verses only reinforces this point. As we said in the previous chapter, we are still in the fourth kingdom, waiting for the kingdom from God.

Now in Chapter 7 verse 19, Daniel tells the angel he wants to know more about the meaning of the fourth beast: "Then I wanted to know the true meaning of the fourth beast, which was different from all the others and most terrifying, with its iron teeth and bronze claws—the beast that crushed and devoured its victims and trampled underfoot whatever was left. I also wanted to know about the ten horns on its head and about the other horn that came up, before which three of them fell—the horn that looked more imposing than the others and that had eyes and a mouth that spoke boastfully. As I watched, this horn was waging war against the saints and defeating them until the Ancient of Days came and pronounced judgment in favor of the saints of the Most High, and the time came when they possessed the kingdom" (Daniel 7:19–22).

Daniel is told about four beasts, but it's the fourth beast that really mystifies and scares him. His request to know more is granted, and he's given a closer look at this terrifying beast:

> The fourth beast is a fourth kingdom that will appear on earth. It will be different from all the other kingdoms and will devour the whole earth, trampling it down and crushing it. The ten horns are ten kings who will come from this kingdom. After them another king will arise, different from the earlier ones; he will subdue three kings. He will speak against the Most High and oppress his saints and try to change the set times and the laws. The saints will be handed over to him for a time, times and half a time.
>
> But the court will sit, and his power will be taken away and completely destroyed forever. Then the sovereignty, power and greatness of the kingdoms under the whole heaven will be handed over to the saints, the people of the Most High. His kingdom will be an everlasting kingdom, and all rulers will worship and obey him. (Daniel 7:23–27)

So what does Daniel's dream from God reveal? What does all of this mean? There are many similarities between Daniel's dream and King Nebuchadnezzar's dream in Chapter 2. Both dreams reveal four empires/kingdoms until the time

God sets up His kingdom, an everlasting divine kingdom. The fourth empire in Chapter 2 is as strong as iron and breaks and crushes all the others; in Chapter 7, it is terrifying and tramples, crushes, and devours the whole earth. In Chapter 2, the fourth kingdom has ten toes of iron mixed with clay; in Chapter 7, the fourth beast has ten horns that are ten kings. However, in Chapter 7, the focus is on the fourth kingdom. Additional information is given to us about some of the rulers and the kingdom's activities. First, we are told there will be ten kings and then an eleventh king who comes to power by subduing three kings. This last king fiercely opposes God and his people. Second, there is a description of God's saints, first being oppressed and defeated for a set amount of time until God intervenes and takes away the power of this last king and then possessing the kingdom of God with "the sovereignty, power and greatness of the kingdoms under the whole heaven … handed over to the saints." This chapter gives deeper insight into the last part of the fourth kingdom, as well as a little more information about a new kingdom—the kingdom of God.

Now, let's place all of this into the affairs of history up to the present, based on what we read in Chapter 2. In the Bible, when the term "beast" is used symbolically, it refers to a false religious system in conjunction with a government. The Bible doesn't label who the beasts are, but there is no reason to believe they are different than the four empires of the statue King Nebuchadnezzar saw. We can speculate the first beast, the lion/eagle, is Babylon and its religious system, and "the heart of a man" may refer to the period in King Nebuchadnezzar's life when he was made to exist like a wild beast to be humbled before God. The second beast, the bear with the three ribs in its mouth, would be the Medo/Persians. The third beast, the leopard with four heads, most likely represents Greece. The four heads probably represent Alexander's empire parceled out to the four winds of the earth after his death. The fourth beast, "different from all the former beasts" would be the Roman Empire, and the ten horns would match the ten toes of iron mixed with clay, the successor kingdoms of the Roman Christian Empire—Europe and the Americas. The Roman Christian Empire is unlike anything seen in Babylon, Medo/Persia, or Greece, because, unlike those empires united under one ruler who controlled both government and religion (many times the ruler was the connection to the deities), it is many nations united by a religion—Christianity. Chapters 2 and 7 reveal only four kingdoms from the time of Daniel's vision to the arrival of the kingdom of the Ancient of Days, and these four empires dominate the world during this time period. In fact, it's worth concentrating on the phrase in verse 23 that says the fourth kingdom will "devour the whole earth, trampling it down and crushing it." What kingdom since Alexander can claim this accomplishment? Can the Chinese (the previous Mongol empire), or the Japanese, or any one nation in Africa or South America? Not even the Ottoman Empire could claim to have devoured the whole earth. The only kingdom that can claim this is the Christian kingdom. To illustrate the point, think of the world at the height of the Spanish Empire around 1550 or the British Empire around 1850, or the American empire in 1945. The Christian kingdom has controlled most of the world's commerce and governments, at different times ruling over all of the Ottoman Empire, the nations of India, China, Japan, Africa, and South America. It has been this way for centuries.

For those living in this kingdom, it's hard to think about the world in this way, but history can produce no other candidate for this position. The Bible also says this fourth kingdom devours the earth, tramples and crushes it. Throughout our history, we have fought adversaries with ideologies that desired world influence such as Totalitarianism, Communism, and militant Islam, but often we are the ones exerting influence on other nations around the world. We view our exertion of influence as helpful, spreading democracy, freedom, and Christianity to others. It's not a secret that the Christian kingdom consumes most of the world's resources, subjugating weaker countries in order to satiate its peoples' needs and wants. It shouldn't be a surprise to us that for those living outside this kingdom, the Christian empire may not be viewed as the benevolent nation that we see. This isn't meant as a political statement or editorial, but a description of what the Bible says the fourth kingdom will look like.

Now let's look at the apocalyptic verse 8 of Chapter 7. Daniel sees a little horn that uproots three of the original ten horns, speaks blasphemy, and persecutes God's saints. In fact, the saints will be handed over to this horn for a set period of time. But it is also during the reign of this horn that Jesus Christ returns, destroys the kingdoms of the earth, and sets up His everlasting kingdom. How does all of this come about? This little horn appears to be some kind of religious/government ruler who comes to power by subduing three other rulers/governments of the Christian kingdom. He becomes very powerful—the only one who brings him down is Jesus Christ Himself. However, this is all we can say about the little horn with the information given here, so we'll have to wait for more information in future chapters.

This vision given to Daniel is quite shocking at the end because it includes the appearance of a ruler who will "speak against the Most High and oppress his saints and try to change the set times and the laws. The saints will be handed over to him for a time, times and half a time." It comes to an end with the Ancient of Days destroying the kingdoms of this world—the only government mankind has ever known—and setting up His kingdom, the kingdom of God. It's no wonder Daniel reacts the way he does in verse 28 of Chapter 7: "This is the end of the matter. I, Daniel, was deeply troubled by my thoughts, and my face turned pale, but I kept the matter to myself." Imagine seeing all of what he had seen, including the throne room of Heaven, the persecution and murder of the saints, the destruction of man's system of government, and the inauguration of God's rule here on earth. This dream was as deeply troubling to Daniel as a similar dream had been to King Nebuchadnezzar.

The good news is that Chapter 7 ends with the return of Jesus Christ who destroys the fourth beast, of which the little horn is part, as well as the three former beasts. He then sets up His kingdom and hands power and authority over to His saints; this is how His everlasting reign on earth begins. Imagine: God ruling the governments here on earth, where His peace, prosperity, and righteousness prevail as the order of the day! Isaiah 9:6, 7 says, "For to us a child is born, to us a son is given, and the government will be on his shoulders. And he will be called Wonderful Counselor, Mighty God, Everlasting Father, Prince of Peace. Of the increase of his government and peace there will be no end. He will reign on David's throne and over his kingdom, establishing and upholding with justice and righteousness from that time on and forever. The zeal of the Lord Almighty will accomplish this."

Before we leave this chapter, we want to reiterate one important point: There are only four empires that rule the earth from the time of Daniel's captivity to the return of Jesus Christ. This means that since Jesus Christ has not yet arrived to set up His everlasting kingdom that He hands over to His saints, we're in one of those four empires. The premise of this book is that we are currently in the last kingdom, under the ten horns of the fourth beast. The ten horns, we believe, represent the "kings" of the Christian empire of Europe and America. The only way to see if this configuration is correct is to watch and see if all that is prophesied in these chapters of the book of Daniel come true. In the next chapter of this book, we'll look at another vision given by God to Daniel. It is from this prophecy that we believe God allows us to see exactly where we are in the last days of the empire of the ten horns.

4

A Ram and a Goat in the Time of Wrath—An End-Time Scenario

We saw in the last chapter that Daniel was especially interested in the fourth kingdom. As the book of Daniel continues, God reveals more detail about that kingdom including the little horn that comes out of the ten horns. God focuses exclusively on these characters in Chapter 8 of Daniel. In this chapter, we will see for the first time what we believe are modern nations identified in events that are occurring right now. We will also see in more detail what's going to happen to these nations in the future and how the "little horn" mentioned in Chapter 7 that "spoke boastfully" will rise to power.

In Chapter 8, we read that Daniel has another vision. This occurs "in the third year of King Belshazzar's reign," two years after the vision of the four beasts in Chapter 7. Daniel says, "I saw myself in the citadel of Susa in the province of Elam; in the vision I was beside the Ulai Canal" (Daniel 8:2). Daniel is taken, in a vision, to the area of what is today southwestern Iran, near the Iraqi border. God purposely brings Daniel to this place because it has meaning. Susa, under the Babylonians, was a center of religious worship, and under the Medes and Persians, it was home to the Zoroastrian pantheon. Many major religions can trace some, or all, of their origins back to this worship center. It is here that God reveals an end-time prophecy about the worshipers of these pagan systems represented in Susa. The book of Revelation in Chapters 17 and 18 talks about this same religious system and calls it by its country of origin—Babylon! It is important to understand what the main focus of the Bible is—worshiping God. God takes worship very seriously: He's let us know how to worship Him, and He's warned us against including the worship traditions of other gods. We have the example of Israel throughout the first part of the Bible, how they turned from worshiping Him and began to include worship to other gods from the people around them. When they turned from doing what God said to do, He turned them over to the gods of wood and stone they were worshiping. (We will read later about the powerful events of Daniel Chapters 3 and 6 that deal directly with true and false worship.)

> I looked up, and there before me was a ram with two horns, standing beside the canal, and the horns were long. One of the horns was longer than the other but grew up later. I watched the ram as he charged toward the west and the north and the south. No animal could stand against him, and none could rescue the ram from his power. He did as he pleased and became great.
>
> As I was thinking about this, suddenly a goat with a prominent horn between his eyes came from the west, crossing the whole earth without touching the ground. He came toward the two-horned ram I had seen standing beside the canal and charged at him in great rage. I saw him attack the ram furiously, striking the ram and shattering his two horns. The ram was powerless to stand against him; the goat knocked him to the ground and trampled on him, and none could rescue the ram from his power. The goat became very great, but at the height of his power his large horn was broken off, and in its place four prominent horns grew up toward the four winds of heaven.
>
> Out of one of them came another horn, which started small but grew in power to the south and to the east and toward the Beautiful Land. It grew until it reached the host of the heavens, and it threw some of the starry host down to the earth and trampled on them. It set itself up to be as great as the Prince of the host; it took away the daily sacrifice from him, and the place of his sanctuary was brought low. Because of rebellion, the host of the saints and the daily sacrifice were given over to it. It prospered in everything it did, and truth was thrown to the ground. (Daniel 8:3–12)

Then Daniel heard angels or God speaking:

> Then I heard a holy one speaking, and another holy one said to him, "How long will it take for the vision to be fulfilled—the vision concerning the daily sacrifice, the rebellion that causes desolation, and the surrender of the sanctuary and of the host that will be trampled underfoot?"
>
> He said to me, "It will take 2,300 evenings and mornings; then the sanctuary will be reconsecrated." (Daniel 8:13, 14)

While Daniel watched the vision, a voice called out (most likely the Word of God who later came as Jesus Christ), "Gabriel, tell this man the meaning of the vision" (verse 16). There are several times in the Bible where the Lord, also known as the Word of God, is with two other beings, most likely the archangels Michael and Gabriel. In the book of Daniel, the two have prominent roles—nowhere else in the Bible do they both receive so much attention. We see that Michael has the role of protector and Gabriel that of herald.

Gabriel approaches Daniel and says, "Son of man, understand that the vision concerns the time of the end." What Gabriel says is incredibly important because it sets the time of these events. This vision is not describing Alexander the Great's demise two hundred years later, as many people believe; this event occurs at the end time. Gabriel repeated when the vision will be fulfilled: "I am going to tell you what will happen later in the time of wrath, because the vision concerns the appointed time of the end" (Daniel 8:19).

The term "time of wrath" is also used in the book of Revelation Chapter 15. This describes a period of time right before the return of Jesus Christ. Gabriel's announcement is an important time marker because it links the time of the end and the time of wrath. If we know when this vision occurs, then we can know where we are in biblical events.

Now that Gabriel has told Daniel the time of this vision, he then tells him the meaning of the vision.

> The two-horned ram that you saw represents the kings of Media and Persia. The shaggy goat is the king of Greece, and the large horn between his eyes is the first king. The four horns that replaced the one that was broken off represent four kingdoms that will emerge from his nation but will not have the same power. (Daniel 8:20–22)

The horn is the symbol of a ruler, as we saw in Chapter 7. The subsequent four horns do not have the same power as the one powerful horn. This is often interpreted as a forecast of the coming Greek empire led by Alexander, the conqueror of Media and Persia. At the height of his power, Alexander died and his kingdom was divided up by his generals. These new kingdoms were not as powerful as Alexander's kingdom had been. However, there are two issues that preclude the vision from being a forecast of Alexander's rise and fall. First, Gabriel says this event will occur at the time of the end, and Alexander's end was 2,333 years ago. I think it is fair to say that 2,333 years ago was not the time of the end. Second, as we shall see, there is the final part of the vision that ushers in a wicked one who is destroyed "but not by human power" (Daniel 8:25). This clearly did not happen after the fall of Alexander. So we need to see if we can find a more accurate modern pattern for this prophecy.

The countries of Media and Persia are today known as Iraq, Iran, and parts of Afghanistan and Jordan. In fact, the Iranians are still referred to as Persians. But who, or what, is Greece? Greece was the first European superpower and the predecessor to Rome. The Romans kept many of the cultural, political, and religious traditions of the Greeks. Greece, with its democratic and Socratic characteristics, can clearly be labeled as the founder of the Western lifestyle we know today. So the term "Greece" could be used in this chapter as the country, or countries, that lead the West. It is fairly obvious the vision doesn't refer to modern-day Greece, which no longer has a prominent military or political role. But who would be a modern successor of Greece? This successor could be a mono power, a nation of great conquest, and the leader of the Western/European world. The vision also tells us that this Greece will come from the west and cross the whole earth without touching the ground. Could the United States of America and its European allies fit the picture? These countries are the leaders of the West and the successor to Alexander's Greece in terms of conquest and prominence. Let's put together a ram and goat scenario using the countries we have identified, encompassing the last thirty or forty years, that might align with the vision and with what we've said in previous chapters.

The two-horned ram is standing beside the Ulai canal in the citadel of Susa—the very center of religious worship for the ancient Medes and Persians. It is possible the ram's location also has a religious connotation attached to it. The ram charges in three directions, north, south, and west, but does not charge east. Beginning in the 1950s and 60s a fundamentalist revival began to take place in Islam. By the 1970s, this movement was becoming a serious problem for Russia, Europe, Africa, and the United States. The Islamic revival spread south, north, and west. In 1978, the Iranian ayatollah overthrew the shah and established an Islamic theocracy in Iran. Iraq, Saudi Arabia, and Syria are at this time the Sunni Moslem centers of power, and Iran is the Shiite center of power. The biggest problem for the West was that the Islamic nations held control over a large portion of the world's precious oil supplies. Iraq, a country with huge oil reserves, was becoming a serious military threat. In 1990, Iraq charged south and invaded Kuwait, and the United States and its Western/European allies crossed the whole earth without touching the ground (moved a large portion of its military by air travel) and pushed Iraq back to its borders. The United States established military bases in Saudi Arabia, Kuwait, and Dubai as a protectorate for these countries. After September 2001, the United States, with a small European coalition, attacked and overthrew the government of Afghanistan and later in 2003, Iraq. As of this writing, the United States is threatening to attack Iran because of its nuclear developments and has warned Syria that it faces attack if it continues to aid and abet terrorists. The vision Daniel receives says that both of the ram's horns will be shattered which seems to suggest the goat may also attack Iran. So, it is quite possible to project this prophecy outward, identifying the kings of Media and Persia as Iraq and Iran, and identifying Greece as the United States and its European allies. It is clear in this scenario that one of the two horns—Iraq—has been kicked to the ground, and, at this writing, the West is threatening to attack Iran.

Now for events in the vision that are still to come. The goat, the nations of the Christian kingdom, and the prominent horn, the United States, will have attacked Iraq and Iran and "knocked him to the ground and trampled on him." But at the height of its power, the goat's horn will be broken off. The subsequent four horns do not have the same power as the one powerful horn. We can look back at what happened to the Greek empire led by Alexander when he conquered Media and Persia to see what happened when another great empire fell and was divided up into smaller permutations. At the height of his power, Alexander died and his kingdom was divided into several new kingdoms. These new areas wielded power, but they were not as powerful as Alexander's kingdom had been. So we see the collapse of the prominent horn is a very important part of end-time prophecy because it leads to the rise of the four smaller horns and ultimately the rise of "a stern-faced king, a master of intrigue." Because we believe this prophecy is describing the events of today, not 2,300 years ago, this would mean the U.S.—the large prominent horn—at the height of its power will somehow fall or collapse (more on this in Chapter 11). Living in the United States, it is hard to imagine the U.S. ceasing to exist as a prominent world power, but it has happened to great nations before: the Soviet Union, Britain, Spain, Rome, Greece, Medo/Persia, Babylon, and Egypt. The U.S. is not immune to what I call "empire atrophy." Besides, if this is what is prophesied by God to happen, it will occur no matter how impossible it may seem.

The loss of U.S. power will certainly affect the Christian empire, but apparently "in its place four prominent horns grew up toward the four winds of heaven." The vacuum will be filled by other nations acting in unison. It's not unrealistic to think of Britain, France, and Germany—the E-3, and the essential European power behind NATO—coming together to maintain the Christian empire. The fourth nation could be the remaining weakened U.S. Whether the U.S. goes bankrupt or suffers some kind of military tragedy, its presence seems too big to completely disappear. Furthermore, when Alexander's empire fell in 323 BC, the empire was divided into four to six smaller kingdoms, and Greece proper was part of the arrangement of those kingdoms. When verse 22 says the four horns are four kingdoms that will emerge from his nation, I believe it means four countries will emerge from the Christian kingdom to replace the lead nation that has fallen. Since World War II, the U.S. has been THE leader of the Christian kingdom; its money, military, and foreign policy have led the way. Everyone in the Christian kingdom has had to follow the U.S., like it or not. After the U.S.'s collapse, a reorganized U.S. with less power, combined with Germany, Britain, and France, seems the most likely candidate at this writing to be the new leader of the western/Christian kingdom, but they will not be as strong a force as the U.S. was before its collapse.

For an unknown period of time, this foursome will maintain order in the Christian kingdom. Verse 23 gives some insight into what happens at the end, or latter part, of the time period when it says: "when the rebels have become completely wicked." The word "wicked" may not just imply moral turpitude, such as violence or sexual behavior. The term wicked may also include the kind of worship God hates (see chapter on worship). It is possible this time period could be one in which many people are still very religious or that religion might experience expansion and growth so that you would actually think society was becoming less wicked. It is just important to remember that wickedness can also imply false worship, so it is hard to know exactly what is meant here. After this time period has come to fulfillment, and the Bible doesn't say how long that will be, a wicked, stern-faced leader will come to the fore.

The angel Gabriel continued the explanation:

> In the latter part of their reign [the four kingdoms mentioned in the previous verse], when rebels have become completely wicked, a stern-faced king, a master of intrigue, will arise. He will become very strong, but not by his own power. He will cause astounding devastation and will succeed in whatever he does. He will destroy the mighty men and the holy people. He will cause deceit to prosper, and he will consider himself superior. When they feel secure, he will destroy many and take his stand against the Prince of princes. Yet he will be destroyed, but not by human power. (Daniel 8:23–25)

The four successors to the large horn maintain a presence for a while, but then a "wicked, stern-faced king, a master of intrigue" rises to power. This leader succeeds in whatever he does—but not by his own power. What does this mean? Whose power does he use? There are a few possibilities. It could mean this person is using someone else's power, like a vicarious ruler or an adviser who rules through a head of state, or it could be talking about another kind of power. This is one of those times when the book of Revelation is helpful because it also gives a description of events at the end time. Chapters 11–19 of Revelation speak of a final, end-time beast that derives his power directly from Satan. Revelation also strongly indicates that this individual will be both a national sovereign and a religious leader just like the rulers of Babylon, Persia, Greece, and Rome experienced. Daniel 8:24, 25 says this king succeeds in whatever he does and causes much destruction. This is the same little horn mentioned in Daniel Chapter 7 that subdues three kings. This final end-time power will come from one of the four who succeed the fallen U.S. There is no indication of which country will produce this little horn, but it seems he will lead some kind of religious movement. Any country, including the U.S., is a contender for host of this new power.

Verse 24 says, "He will destroy the mighty men and the holy people." This explains verse 11 where this leader "took away the daily sacrifice ... and the place of [God's] sanctuary was brought low ... the host of the saints and the daily sacrifice were given over to [him]." The people with the Spirit of God are God's sanctuary, as it says in I Corinthians 3:16, 17: "Don't you know that you yourselves are God's temple and that God's Spirit lives in you? If anyone destroys God's temple, God will destroy him; for God's temple is sacred, and you are that temple." King David says in Psalm 141:2, "May my prayer be set before you like incense; may the lifting up of my hands be like the evening sacrifice." This final power kills and destroys those God has called to worship Him. Revelation 13:5–8 describes a similar situation: "The beast was given a mouth to utter proud words and blasphemies and to exercise his authority for forty-two months. He opened his mouth to blaspheme God, and to slander his name and his dwelling place and those who live in heaven. He was given power to make war against the saints and to conquer them. And he was given authority over every tribe, people, language and nation. All inhabitants of the earth will worship the beast—all whose names have not been written in the book of life belonging to the Lamb that was slain from the creation of the world." We are told in Daniel the persecution will last 2,300 mornings and evenings, or 1,150 days. This stern-faced king tries to wipe out all truth and sets himself up to be equal to Jesus Christ (Daniel 8:11).

It seems that this stern-faced king sets himself up as the secular ruler and then takes power as the religious ruler (verses 9–11). The Bible indicates *many* people, "all inhabitants of the earth," will feel this stern-faced king is doing the right thing (Daniel 8:25; 11:24)—they'll believe it's the right path for them and their country. When verse 24 states the king goes against God by destroying the "holy people" and ultimately takes a stand against the Prince of princes, we need to remember that anything against God is from Satan. Satan's greatest tool is deception—It's how he flourishes, and in this case, it is how the stern-faced king rises to the zenith of his power. People will believe what he does is good, even godly, but it will be quite the contrary. The Bible says there will be a group of people who know what this little horn represents (Daniel 11:32), and when they are told to worship this king, they will refuse just like Shadrach, Meshach, and Abednego. They will be imprisoned or sent to their deaths because of their fealty to God. This is what is described when it says he will destroy the mighty men and the holy people, and because they are destroyed, all truth will be thrown to the ground and deceit will prosper. A severe persecution is coming on those who follow the truth, but we'll discuss that later.

The little horn takes "his stand against the Prince of princes," or Jesus Christ. But there is one line of good news Gabriel gives right at the end of his explanation: "Yet he [the wicked king] will be destroyed, but not by human power." The little horn, the stern-faced king, a master of intrigue, is destroyed, not by some righteous group of people who overthrow him, but by the only other power left—God's power. Jesus Christ will return to destroy this final kingdom set up by Satan. (Remember the stone that destroyed the final kingdom in the statue?) It is important to note that God allows this ruler to exist. Just as God hardened Pharaoh's heart back in Egypt for his own purpose, He will allow this government to rule for His own purpose as well.

When Gabriel was finished explaining the vision to Daniel, he told him, "The vision of the evenings and mornings that has been given you is true ..." Evenings and mornings were a time when the Israelites performed daily sacrifices at the temple in Jerusalem, the place where God placed his name. Finally, Gabriel tells Daniel, "... but seal up the vision, for it concerns the distant future" (Daniel 8:26).

God didn't reveal any more information because understanding was to come at a later time—the time of the end. This vision was for a time over 2,500 years later, not a mere two hundred years as some have speculated. Daniel says it was so shocking he was exhausted and sick in bed for several days after. "I was appalled by the vision; it was beyond understanding." Daniel was emotionally drained from the whole experience. The vision itself must have been much more shocking than what we read. Daniel had been around war, seen people put to death, and watched his nation taken into captivity by a brutal nation, so it wasn't as though Daniel had lived a soft, protected life. Seeing this vision must have been horrifying and beyond the pale of anything he could have ever imagined. Daniel, for all that he knew, was unable to understand the vision because so many concepts and events were beyond what he had known and understood.

This is the last vision Daniel records while he's in the kingdom of Babylon. After this, as we read in Chapter 5, Cyrus/Darius conquers the Babylonians and Daniel becomes a counselor under the Medes.

The vision of Chapter 8 is part of a series of revelations that are insights into the events and chronology of the Gentile kingdoms. However, in Chapter 8, God chooses to focus in on the last part of the Gentile rule, the time of wrath just before the arrival of Jesus Christ. Daniel receives a more focused picture of what he asked for in Chapter 7: to know more about the fourth beast, its ten horns, and the other horn that came up and subdued three—the horn that looked more imposing than the others and had eyes and a mouth that spoke boastfully. Chapter 8 reveals that the little horn derives its power from Satan, that this beast will rise to power by deceit and cunning means, and that the only way to destroy the power of the little horn/beast power is through the arrival of Jesus Christ and His saints. It is somewhat unsettling to see biblical prophecy unfold before your eyes in modern times—it is much more comfortable to look back and see what has been prophesied and fulfilled, especially when it's in antiquity. But these prophecies are assigned for the time of the end; in fact, a fairly large portion of biblical prophecy is dedicated to the last days. Perhaps because so few mainstream churches talk about prophecy in the present and future, it has become a strange and uncomfortable topic. It's much easier to talk about Isaiah's prophecy of Christ's birth year after year, as though that was the only prophecy God gave us in scripture, and since it's already happened, it creates little controversy. But even if this book's predictions about specific countries are incorrect, at some point, some country, some individual(s) will fulfill God's revelation to Daniel. At some point, the "little horn" will wage war against the saints of God and will overcome them and destroy them, but in the end, the "stern-faced king, a master of intrigue" will be destroyed, not by human power, but by the "rock cut out of the mountain, but not by human hands."

5

Worship and Rulership

So far, we have covered three chapters in the book of Daniel that describe kingdoms and kings that exist up to the end of the age. These kingdoms all have one thing in common: They worship gods of wood and stone. But there are other chapters in Daniel that describe the events of people who worship the true God, and it's usually by refusing to worship false gods. Above all else, the Bible is a book about God. It's where He explains who He is, the Supreme Power who created all things; how to worship Him; and what He plans to do. The Bible is full of examples of men and women, and nations, who worshiped God, as well as those who didn't. In the second chapter of the very first book in the Bible, God teaches Adam, whom He just created, about worshiping Him. He sets in motion laws designed by omniscient wisdom, and here He gives Adam a choice: worship God through obedience, or sin against God through disobedience. "You are free to eat from any tree in the garden," God tells Adam, "but you must not eat from the tree of the knowledge of good and evil, for when you eat of it you will surely die" (Genesis 2:16). Adam chose not to worship God, and death became a reality for human beings. God warns Adam's son Cain, regarding his offering to God, "If you do what is right, will you not be accepted? But if you do not do what is right, sin is crouching at your door; it desires to have you, but you must master it" (Genesis 4:7). Cain chose not to worship God.

Generations later, the state of mankind had deteriorated to the point that "The Lord saw how great man's wickedness on the earth had become, and that every inclination of the thoughts of his heart was only evil all the time" (Genesis 6:5). But there was one man who worshiped God: "But Noah found favor in the eyes of the Lord ... Noah was a righteous man, blameless among the people of his time, and he walked with God" (Genesis 6:8, 9). Noah chose to worship God, and because of that, he and his family were the only people saved from the flood. And then there was a man about whose act of obedience we have already read, an act that affects you and me and all of mankind: Abraham's obedience to God's command to sacrifice his son—the son God had miraculously given him, the son who was to be his heir, the son through whom descendents as numerous as the stars and sand were promised, the son who would inhabit the land around Abraham as far as he could see. With all this in mind, Abraham still obeyed God.

> "The fire and wood are here," Isaac said, "but where is the lamb for the burnt offering?"
> Abraham answered, "God himself will provide the lamb for the burnt offering, my son."

And God did. He held Abraham back from offering Isaac and provided a ram caught in a nearby bush. "I swear by myself, declares the Lord, that because you have done this and have not withheld your son, your only son, I will surely bless you and make your descendants as numerous as the stars in the sky and as the sand on the seashore. Your descendants will take possession of the cities of their enemies, and through your offspring all nations on earth will be blessed, because you have obeyed me."

Obedience comes through faith in God—believing that God is who He says He is and that He will do what He says He'll do. Hebrews 11:1 says, "Now faith is being sure of what we hope for and certain of what we do not see." The rest of the chapter lists men and women who faithfully obeyed God, even in times of trouble and at their own peril. In Hebrews 12:28, the final exhortation is, "Therefore, since we are receiving a kingdom that cannot be shaken"—the kingdom set up by God—"let us be thankful, and so worship God acceptably with reverence and awe, for our 'God is a consuming fire.'" This verse quotes Deuteronomy 4:23, 24, where Moses says to the Israelites, "Be careful not to forget the covenant of the Lord your God that he made with you; do not make for yourselves an idol in the form of anything the Lord your God has forbidden. For the Lord your God is a consuming fire, a jealous God." God describes Himself as a jealous God many times throughout the Bible, always in conjunction with His people worshiping other gods. When God gave the commandments to Israel, He said, "You shall not make for yourself an idol in the form of anything in heaven above or on the earth beneath or in the waters below. You shall not bow down to them or worship them; for I, the Lord your God, am a jealous God, punishing the children for the sin of the fathers to the third and fourth generation of those who hate me, but showing love to a thousand generations of those who love me and keep my commandments" (Exodus 20:4–6). Again to the Israelites, God says, "Be careful not to make a treaty with those who live in the land where you are going, or they will be a snare among you. Break down their altars, smash their sacred stones and cut down their Asherah poles. Do not worship any other god, for the Lord, whose name is Jealous, is a jealous God" (Exodus 34:12–14).

Moses reminds God's people again, "Fear the Lord your God, serve him only and take your oaths in his name. Do not follow other gods, the gods of the peoples around you; for the Lord your God, who is among you, is a jealous God and his anger will burn against you, and he will destroy you from the face of the land" (Deuteronomy 6:13–15). The command to God's people is clear: don't worship the gods and idols around you—worship the one true God through obedience. It's a matter of eternal life and death.

The book of Daniel contains many prophecies, but every chapter includes the subject of worship. This brings us to Daniel Chapter One, the book begins with Nebuchadnezzar, king of Babylon, attacking Jerusalem. God is involved in the event—He orchestrates the captivity of His people. "The Lord delivered Jehoiakim king of Judah into [Nebuchadnezzar's] hand, along with some of the articles from the temple of God. These he carried off to the temple of his god in Babylonia and put in the treasure house of his god" (Daniel 1:2). The king brought "some of the Israelites from the royal family and the nobility—young men without any physical defect, handsome, showing aptitude for every kind of learning, well informed, quick to understand, and qualified to serve in the king's palace." These young men would be taught "the language and literature of the Babylonians. The king assigned them a daily amount of food and wine from the king's table. They were to be trained for three years, and after that they were to enter the king's service" (verses 3–5). It is here we are introduced to four young men of the tribe of Judah: Daniel, Hananiah, Mishael, and Azariah. The last three are more famously known by their Babylonian names Shadrach, Meshach, and Abednego.

A point of conflict has now been set up: Many Israelite men who know the true God are brought to a foreign country with foreign gods of wood and stone. They'll be trained in the language, literature, history, and religion of a people who do not know the true God.

Verse 8 describes how four of the young men handle being in a land with foreign gods: "But Daniel resolved not to defile himself with the royal food and wine, and he asked the chief official for permission not to defile himself in this way." The food and wine from the king's table went against the dietary laws God had given his people in the scriptures. It is interesting that all of the other young men from Israel ate from the king's table; only Daniel, Hananiah, Mishael, and Azariah are noted as having the resolve not to break God's law. They had the faith to obey, or worship, God. God's desire is that we always put him first—"Love the Lord your God with all your heart and with all your soul and with all your mind" (Matthew 22:37).

> Now God had caused the official to show favor and sympathy to Daniel, but the official told Daniel, "I am afraid of my lord the king, who has assigned you food and drink. Why should he see you looking worse than the other young men your age? The king would then have my head because of you."

Daniel could have stopped here and said, "Well, at least I tried!" But he continued to press the issue:

> Daniel then said to the guard whom the chief official had appointed over Daniel, Hananiah, Mishael and Azariah, "Please test your servants for ten days: Give us nothing but vegetables to eat and water to drink. Then compare our appearance with that of the young men who eat the royal food, and treat your servants in accordance with what you see." So he agreed to this and tested them for ten days.
> At the end of the ten days they looked healthier and better nourished than any of the young men who ate the royal food. So the guard took away their choice food and the wine they were to drink and gave them vegetables instead.
> To these four young men God gave knowledge and understanding of all kinds of literature and learning. And Daniel could understand visions and dreams of all kinds.
> At the end of the time set by the king to bring them in, the chief official presented them to Nebuchadnezzar. The king talked with them, and he found none equal to Daniel, Hananiah, Mishael and Azariah; so they entered the king's service. In every matter of wisdom and understanding about which the king questioned them, he found them ten times better than all the magicians and enchanters in his whole kingdom.

Because these four men were obedient to God, He blessed them. God—who created everything—gave them knowledge and understanding; it shouldn't be surprising that a human king found the men ten times better than his own experienced staff. God singled Daniel out and gave him a special gift: the ability to understand visions and dreams. This understanding of dreams and visions saved the lives of Daniel, his friends, and the other wise men serving the king, and it was also the way in which God revealed future nations and events to his people at the end time. The whole book of Daniel is the result of a gift that came as a blessing for worshiping God.

In the third chapter of Daniel, another choice to worship the true God or worship gods of wood and stone arises. The chapter opens with King Nebuchadnezzar unveiling an image of gold ninety feet high and nine feet wide. A proclamation is sent out to the officials in Babylon: "As soon as you hear the sound of the horn, flute, zither, lyre, harp, pipes and all kinds of music, you must fall down and worship the image of gold that King Nebuchadnezzar has set up. Whoever does not fall down and worship will immediately be thrown into a blazing furnace." And so when everyone heard those musical instruments play "all the peoples, nations and men of every language fell down and worshiped the image of gold that Nebuchadnezzar had set up." Who wouldn't choose to worship this image with the penalty of instant death hanging over his head? Nebuchadnezzar was the undisputed king over the area and, as people saw it, his gods were the ones who had delivered victory to Babylon so his gods were the ones to worship.

As the command went out, the expectation was that all would obey; however, as we see in verses 8–12, not everyone did. Shadrach, Meshach, and Abednego refused to bow down to the king's image of gold. These three were aware they were not Babylonian; they were Jewish men taken from Israel and put into positions of authority by the very same king who now commanded them to worship this image. But Shadrach, Meshach, and Abednego knew God, knew how to worship Him, and knew He hated idolatry. They understood that when you know who God is, you worship only Him.

So the music sounded, and quickly everyone bowed low and worshiped the image. Maybe it was loyalty to the king or jealousy, but whatever the motive, some astrologers who served the king took notice and reported that Shadrach, Meshach, and Abednego did not bow down and worship the image. In fact, they reported these three didn't worship any of the gods of Babylon. The astrologers also reminded the king of the punishment he decreed: Whoever didn't bow down to worship the ninety-foot idol would be thrown into a blazing furnace. The king reacted with rage! He immediately ordered Shadrach, Meshach, and Abednego to appear before him for questioning. The king asked: "Is it true, Shadrach, Meshach, and Abednego, that you do not serve my gods or worship the image of gold I have set up?" Before they could answer the king, he gave them a second chance by repeating his command. He told them again that when they heard the sound of all kinds of music, they must fall down and worship the image, and all would be well. "But if you do not worship it, you will be thrown immediately into a blazing furnace." Then King Nebuchadnezzar boasted about the strength of his god, which he saw as obvious from past experience: "Then what god will be able to rescue you from my hand?" The king believed his god was stronger than their God.

What follows is one of the most incredible demonstrations of faithful worship in the Bible. The answer from Shadrach, Meshach, and Abednego was firm: "O Nebuchadnezzar, we do not need to defend ourselves before you in this matter. If we are thrown into the blazing furnace, the God we serve is able to save us from it, and he will rescue us from your hand, O king." Now comes the most astonishing part of their response: "But even if he does not, we want you to know, O king, that we will not serve your gods or worship the image of gold you have set up." They tell the king—to his face—they will only worship God whether He saves them or not; they are firm in their obedience to God and it's not contingent on His response.

Again the king responded with *great* rage! He ordered the furnace to be heated seven times hotter than usual and ordered his strongest soldiers to apprehend and tie up the troika! They were still wearing their robes, trousers, and turbans when they were thrown into the blazing furnace. Because the fire was so hot and they had little time to safely prepare the execution, the soldiers who threw Shadrach, Meshach, and Abednego into the furnace were instantly killed by the heat of the fire. The three men, firmly bound, tumbled into the blazing inferno. Nebuchadnezzar confidently believed his gods were stronger.

But Nebuchadnezzar was about to learn of the God who was able to rescue His people from the king's hand, the God of Abraham, Isaac, Jacob, and Shadrach, Meshach, and Abednego. After the men were thrown into the furnace,

> King Nebuchadnezzar leaped to his feet in amazement and asked his advisors, "Weren't there three men that we tied up and threw into the fire?"
>
> They replied, "Certainly, O king."
>
> He said, "Look! I see four men walking around in the fire, unbound and unharmed, and the fourth looks like a son of the gods." Nebuchadnezzar then approached the opening of the blazing furnace and shouted, "Shadrach, Meshach and Abednego, servants of the Most High God, come out! Come here!"
>
> So Shadrach, Meshach and Abednego came out of the fire, and the satraps, prefects, governors and royal advisers crowded around them. They saw that the fire had not harmed their bodies, nor was a hair of their heads singed; their robes were not scorched, and there was no smell of fire on them.
>
> Then Nebuchadnezzar said, "Praise be to the God of Shadrach, Meshach and Abednego, who has sent his angel and rescued his servants! They trusted in him and defied the king's command and were willing to give up their lives rather than serve or worship any god except their own God. Therefore I decree

that the people of any nation or language who say anything against the God of Shadrach, Meshach and Abednego be cut into pieces and their houses be turned into piles of rubble, for no other god can save in this way."

Then the king promoted Shadrach, Meshach and Abednego in the province of Babylon.

These three young men trusted in God and were willing to give up their lives rather than worship another god. This same kind of worship will be required of those who know God in the end time, as we shall see later in the book of Daniel. As Jesus Christ says in Luke 17:33, "Whoever tries to keep his life will lose it, and whoever loses his life will preserve it." Daniel Chapter 3 is a prophetic window on what life will be like when God's people are given over to the final king of Chapter 8. At that time, when people are told to worship the "little horn—the stern-faced master of intrigue," those who love God will say, "Our God will rescue us, but even if He doesn't, we are not worshiping you or your gods." Because of their faithful worship, they will lose their lives, but only for a short while—We'll pick up the rest of the story when we cover Daniel Chapter 11.

Before we go any further, I think it's worth asking, where was Daniel during all of this? I'm sure he wasn't bowing down to the idol, so why wasn't he part of the story? We're left with pure speculation, but the answer may reside with those who ratted out the three men—the astrologers. Remember back in Chapter 2 when Nebuchadnezzar had the dream of the statue and he wanted his astrologers to tell him the dream and then interpret it? Because the astrologers could not tell the king his dream, he was going to cut them into pieces and turn their houses into piles of rubble. Just when the astrologers were about to be put to death, Daniel intervened and eventually told the king his dream and interpreted it for him. This saved the lives of the astrologers, and because they owed Daniel an enormous debt of gratitude, it's possible that if they knew Daniel didn't worship the image, they turned a blind eye to him. Or perhaps the incident happened so fast Daniel didn't know about the danger to his friends until after the fact, unable to intervene on their behalf. Or maybe he was away on state business. Since the Bible doesn't say, we don't know for sure. But from the accounts we read in the book of Daniel, we can be certain he also didn't worship the image.

There is one other point I want to talk about before we leave Chapter 3—the astrologers. In Babylon, they were also known as "magi." This term should sound familiar to most people because these are the same magi, or wise men, mentioned in the book of Matthew hundreds of years later. A group of magi traveled west to visit another king and bring Him gifts, but we'll talk more about that when we discuss the incredible prophecy given in Daniel Chapter 9.

We now turn to Daniel Chapter 4. This is the only place in the Bible where God has a Gentile king (or any Gentile for that matter) write an entire chapter. King Nebuchadnezzar begins the chapter addressed to all people by praising the true God. This chapter is an account of how God worked with the king to teach him who the true God is. (It's much like the apostle Paul's calling on the road to Damascus as recorded in Acts 9.)

Chapter 4 begins with an address by King Nebuchadnezzar:

> King Nebuchadnezzar,
> To the peoples, nations and men of every language, who live in all the world:
> May you prosper greatly!
> It is my pleasure to tell you about the miraculous signs and wonders that the Most High God has performed for me.
> How great are his signs, how mighty his wonders! His kingdom is an eternal kingdom; his dominion endures from generation to generation. (Daniel 4:1–3)

The king then recounts the series of events that led him to make such a proclamation. It all began when he was describing his pleasure and contentment with the state of his empire. But then he had a dream "that made me afraid. As I was lying in my bed, the images and visions that passed through my mind terrified me" (verse 5). Once again, the king called all the wise men of Babylon to interpret the dream; however, the astrologers, magicians, enchanters, and diviners were unable to interpret the dream. Finally, King Nebuchadnezzar called upon Daniel to interpret the dream. We see throughout Chapter 4, there is an interesting use of names. Before the event happened, Nebuchadnezzar had referred to Daniel as "Belteshazzar," the name he had given him "after the name of my god," but as the king *retells* the story, he refers to Daniel by his Jewish name, acknowledging the God of Daniel.

In verse 9, the king addresses Daniel by acknowledging the gift God has given him—He knows this man has a relationship with God unlike anyone else. The king goes on to relate his terrifying dream, knowing with confidence that Daniel will be able to interpret it.

> "These are the visions I saw while lying in my bed: I looked, and there before me stood a tree in the middle of the land. Its height was enormous. The tree grew large and strong and its top touched the sky; it was visible to the ends of the earth. Its leaves were beautiful, its fruit abundant, and on it was food for all. Under it the beasts of the field found shelter, and the birds of the air lived in its branches; from it every creature was fed.

"In the visions I saw while lying in my bed, I looked, and there before me was a messenger, a holy one, coming down from heaven. He called in a loud voice: 'Cut down the tree and trim off its branches; strip off its leaves and scatter its fruit. Let the animals flee from under it and the birds from its branches. But let the stump and its roots, bound with iron and bronze, remain in the ground, in the grass of the field.

"'Let him be drenched with the dew of heaven, and let him live with the animals among the plants of the earth. Let his mind be changed from that of a man and let him be given the mind of an animal, till seven times pass by for him.

"'The decision is announced by messengers, the holy ones declare the verdict, so that the living may know that the Most High is sovereign over the kingdoms of men and gives them to anyone he wishes and sets over them the lowliest of men.'

"This is the dream that I, King Nebuchadnezzar, had. Now, Belteshazzar, tell me what it means, for none of the wise men in my kingdom can interpret it for me. But you can, because the spirit of the holy gods is in you." (Daniel 4:10–18)

But this dream perplexed Daniel for a while ... and ultimately terrified him! He realized it was bad news for King Nebuchadnezzar, and Daniel had come to have a close relationship with the king. In addition, no one wants to tell his or her boss bad news—especially if your boss has the power to put you to death. The king encouraged Daniel, saying, "Belteshazzar, do not let the dream or its meaning alarm you" (verse 19).

Belteshazzar answered, "My lord, if only the dream applied to your enemies and its meaning to your adversaries! The tree you saw, which grew large and strong, with its top touching the sky, visible to the whole earth, with beautiful leaves and abundant fruit, providing food for all, giving shelter to the beasts of the field, and having nesting places in its branches for the birds of the air—you, O king, are that tree! You have become great and strong; your greatness has grown until it reaches the sky, and your dominion extends to distant parts of the earth."

What Daniel was about to say then took faith in God. Belteshazzar, named after King Nebuchadnezzar's god, was about to tell the king that the God of Israel was going to take his power and kingdom away for "seven times."

"You, O king, saw a messenger, a holy one, coming down from heaven and saying, 'Cut down the tree and destroy it, but leave the stump, bound with iron and bronze, in the grass of the field, while its roots remain in the ground.

Let him be drenched with the dew of heaven; let him live like the wild animals, until seven times pass by for him.'

"This is the interpretation, O king, and this is the decree the Most High has issued against my lord the king: You will be driven away from people and will live with the wild animals; you will eat grass like cattle and be drenched with the dew of heaven. Seven times will pass by for you until you acknowledge that the Most High is sovereign over the kingdoms of men and gives them to anyone he wishes. The command to leave the stump of the tree with its roots means that your kingdom will be restored to you when you acknowledge that Heaven rules. Therefore, O king, be pleased to accept my advice: Renounce your sins by doing what is right, and your wickedness by being kind to the oppressed. It may be that then your prosperity will continue." (Daniel 4:25–27)

Daniel told the king that God would do this to him until he acknowledged that God ruled over the kingdoms and gave them to whomever He wanted. And this is one of the main revelations in the book of Daniel: God gives the kingdoms of men to anyone He wishes—Babylon, Persia, Greece, and Rome. He then sets up His kingdom, the kingdom of God.

King Nebuchadnezzar did not heed Daniel's advice to change, and so:

All this happened to King Nebuchadnezzar. Twelve months later, as the king was walking on the roof of the royal palace of Babylon, he said, "Is not this the great Babylon I have built as the royal residence, by my mighty power and for the glory of my majesty?"

The words were still on his lips when a voice came from heaven, "This is what is decreed for you, King Nebuchadnezzar: Your royal authority has been taken from you. You will be driven away from people and will live with the wild animals; you will eat grass like cattle. Seven times will pass by for you until you acknowledge that the Most High is sovereign over the kingdoms of men and gives them to anyone he wishes."

Immediately what had been said about Nebuchadnezzar was fulfilled. He was driven away from people and ate grass like cattle. His body was drenched with the dew of heaven until his hair grew like the feathers of an eagle and his nails like the claws of a bird. (Daniel 4:28–33)

At that very moment, the king's dream—the one Daniel had interpreted a year earlier—was fulfilled. King Nebuchadnezzar, the greatest and most powerful ruler on earth, was driven from his throne and his people, and lived in the fields and forests eating grass like cattle. His hair grew to cover his body, and his nails were like a bird's claws. He lost his sanity, becoming a madman living in the woods like an animal. God showed the king He controls everything, even our physical and mental health. He took away Nebuchadnezzar's sanity and reduced him to as close to an animal as a human could possibly be. King Nebuchadnezzar was going to learn what Daniel already knew: God does what He says He will do, and He has control over everything. We also should acknowledge this, as King Nebuchadnezzar finally does.

> At the end of that time, I, Nebuchadnezzar, raised my eyes toward heaven, and my sanity was restored. Then I praised the Most High; I honored and glorified him who lives forever.
>
> His dominion is an eternal dominion; his kingdom endures from generation to generation. All the peoples of the earth are regarded as nothing. He does as he pleases with the powers of heaven and the peoples of the earth. No one can hold back his hand or say to him: "What have you done?"
>
> At the same time that my sanity was restored, my honor and splendor were returned to me for the glory of my kingdom. My advisers and nobles sought me out, and I was restored to my throne and became even greater than before. Now I, Nebuchadnezzar, praise and exalt and glorify the King of heaven, because everything he does is right and all his ways are just. And those who walk in pride he is able to humble. (Daniel 4:34–37)

The king finally acknowledged that God has power over everything, even the kingdoms of the world. Upon encountering the true God, King Nebuchadnezzar's response was to worship Him.

When you read this prayer of praise, it's worth remembering this is not an Israelite king or a Levitical priest, but a Gentile king who subdued and conquered God's people. God, when He was angry with Israel, would often say that if He revealed Himself and intervened on behalf of the Gentile nations, they would repent and be far more loyal and faithful than Israel. Jesus Christ said: "Woe to you, Korazin! Woe to you, Bethsaida! [Israelite cities] For if the miracles that were performed in you had been performed in Tyre and Sidon [Gentile cities], they would have repented long ago, sitting in sackcloth and ashes. But it will be more bearable for Tyre and Sidon at the judgment than for you. And you, Capernaum [an Israelite city], will you be lifted up to the skies? No, you will go down to the depths" (Luke 10:13–15).

It's interesting to note that while King Nebuchadnezzar is absent from the throne, no one rushes in to fill the vacuum. In most situations, the king's absence would be followed by some kind of coup, or the next in line would justify succession. Even the United States' Constitution lays out the protocol for who succeeds the president when he is incapacitated. Who knew the king was going to return to sanity, and who probably ran Babylon when the king was out of his mind? The answer to both questions is Daniel. This calls for some speculation, but the Bible tells us the king returned to his throne when his sanity returned, and he didn't have to overthrow someone to do it—his advisors and nobles "sought [him] out." Daniel knew the king's condition was temporary and probably let the royal court know he'd be back. Meanwhile, since Daniel was ruler of the province of Babylon and in charge of all its wise men (Daniel 2:48), he most likely kept things intact and held any would-be successors at bay. Of course, God had no small role in all of this; since the prophecy came from Him and it included King Nebuchadnezzar's return, God made sure everything came to pass.

Think about how great God is! He destroyed Israel and gave them over to a Gentile nation. Then He raised some of His people to high positions within the government, and He gave the king dreams only His servant could interpret. God then set in motion events that resulted in Daniel, the exile from Israel, running the most powerful nation on earth (much like the events of Joseph in Egypt). In the end, it was really King Nebuchadnezzar who was conquered now that he recognized and worshiped the God of Abraham, Isaac, and Israel (Jacob), something many of the kings of Israel were unable to do.

The end of Chapter 4 is the last we hear from King Nebuchadnezzar. History records that he died October of 562 BC after a successful forty-three-year reign over a prosperous period in the Babylonian kingdom. This account of King Nebuchadnezzar is similar to what happened in the short but insightful book of Jonah. Jonah, an Israelite, was consumed by nationalism; he thought God loved only Israel. But God showed Jonah He cared about the Gentile, pagan city of Nineveh as well—He sent Jonah to warn the people to repent and avoid impending destruction. God cares for all the people He's created—"and through your seed all nations on earth will be blessed." This is why He sent His son Jesus Christ into the world, to save Israelites and Gentiles alike from sin and its ultimate penalty: death. There are some who may wonder why God would allow a pagan king to write a chapter of praise in the Bible. I would suggest the very words of King Nebuchadnezzar in his praise of God as an explanation to that question: "All the peoples of the earth are regarded as nothing. He does as he pleases with the powers of heaven and the peoples of the earth. No one can hold back his hand or say to him: 'What have you done?'" God is in charge and He can do what He wants—"everything he does is right and all his ways are just."

Now we come to the rule of King Nebuchadnezzar's son in Chapter 5. His first son to reign was Amel-marduk from 562 to 560 BC when he died. His next son, Belshazzar, is the focus of Chapter 5. Royalty is always about succession—Who's next in line for the throne? King Nebuchadnezzar probably spent most of his time grooming Amel-marduk to succeed him, but it's Belshazzar who ends up ruling the Babylonian Empire. Because Belshazzar didn't have to focus on the responsibility of leadership, he probably lived a hedonistic, playboy life-style, and when he suddenly came to power, he continued to live the same way.

Belshazzar must have been familiar with the story of how his father became like an animal, eating grass and living in the wild until he acknowledged the true God. But Belshazzar obviously didn't learn from his father's lesson. Instead, he specifically commanded his servants to bring in the goblets that had been in God's temple in Jerusalem, and he used them at his party to drink wine while praising and thanking *his* gods of wood and stone. His gods were unaware of what he was doing, but the true God wasn't.

Chapter 5 opens up with King Belshazzar hosting a huge banquet for his nobles:

> King Belshazzar gave a great banquet for a thousand of his nobles and drank wine with them. While Belshazzar was drinking his wine, he gave orders to bring in the gold and silver goblets that Nebuchadnezzar his father had taken from the temple in Jerusalem, so that the king and his nobles, his wives and his concubines might drink from them. So they brought in the gold goblets that had been taken from the temple of God in Jerusalem, and the king and his nobles, his wives and his concubines drank from them. As they drank the wine, they praised the gods of gold and silver, of bronze, iron, wood and stone.
>
> Suddenly, the fingers of a human hand appeared and wrote on the plaster of the wall, near the lamp stand in the royal palace. The king watched the hand as it wrote. His face turned pale and he was so frightened that his knees knocked together and his legs gave way.
>
> The king called out for the enchanters, astrologers and diviners to be brought and said to these wise men of Babylon, "Whoever reads this writing and tells me what it means will be clothed in purple and have a gold chain placed around his neck, and he will be made the third highest ruler in the kingdom."
>
> Then all the king's wise men came in, but they could not read the writing or tell the king what it meant. So King Belshazzar became even more terrified and his face grew more pale. His nobles were baffled.
>
> The queen [or queen mother], hearing the voices of the king and his nobles, came into the banquet hall. "O king, live forever!" she said. "Don't be alarmed! Don't look so pale! There is a man in your kingdom who has the spirit of the holy gods in him. In the time of your father he was found to have insight and intelligence and wisdom like that of the gods. King Nebuchadnez-zar your father—your father the king, I say—appointed him chief of the magi-cians, enchanters, astrologers and diviners. This man Daniel, whom the king

called Belteshazzar, was found to have a keen mind and knowledge and understanding, and also the ability to interpret dreams, explain riddles and solve difficult problems. Call for Daniel, and he will tell you what the writing means."

How could it be that Daniel had gone from ruler over the province of Babylon, in charge of all of the wise men during King Nebuchadnezzar's reign, to an unknown administrator by those in his son's administration? Think of all the great things Daniel did during King Nebuchadnezzar's time—He was essentially the king's right-hand advisor, and most likely the vicarious king while Nebuchadnezzar was incapacitated. There is no doubt Belshazzar knew who Daniel was. (Daniel 5:22 says, "But you his son, O Belshazzar, have not humbled yourself, though you knew all this.") Why, then, wasn't Daniel part of the new king's court? Why did the queen mother have to remind her son of events during his father's reign and about his father's most trusted advisor? It seems that sometimes children of great leaders have a very difficult time living in the shadow of their famous parent. Many feel neglected; they have trouble finding their own identity and feeling secure with that identity. Many times, the children become resentful, jealous, or even hateful towards their parent. With this in mind, it's not too hard to imagine Belshazzar, upon ascending to the throne, dismissing anything and everything that had to do with King Nebuchadnezzar. Whether it was successful or not, if it had to do with his father, it was not going to be part of his reign. But now Belshazzar was desperate and needed someone ... anyone.

> So Daniel was brought before the king, and the king said to him, "Are you Daniel, one of the exiles my father the king brought from Judah? I have heard that the spirit of the gods is in you and that you have insight, intelligence and outstanding wisdom. The wise men and enchanters were brought before me to read this writing and tell me what it means, but they could not explain it. Now I have heard that you are able to give interpretations and to solve difficult problems. If you can read this writing and tell me what it means, you will be clothed in purple and have a gold chain placed around your neck, and you will be made the third highest ruler in the kingdom."
> Then Daniel answered the king, "You may keep your gifts for yourself and give your rewards to someone else. Nevertheless, I will read the writing for the king and tell him what it means." (Daniel 5:1–17)

Daniel's response to this king was much different than to King Nebuchadnezzar. Remember what Daniel said after the king related the dream of the great tree that was later cut down? "My lord, if only the dream applied to your enemies and its meaning to your adversaries!" (Daniel 4:19). But this new king had a different attitude, and he purposely didn't have a relationship with Daniel. Daniel continued:

> "O king, the Most High God gave your father Nebuchadnezzar sovereignty and greatness and glory and splendor. Because of the high position he gave him, all the peoples and nations and men of every language dreaded and feared him. Those the king wanted to put to death, he put to death; those he wanted to spare, he spared; those he wanted to promote, he promoted; and those he wanted to humble, he humbled. But when his heart became arrogant and hardened with pride, he was deposed from his royal throne and stripped of his glory. He was driven away from people and given the mind of an animal; he lived with the wild donkeys and ate grass like cattle; and his body was drenched with the dew of heaven, until he acknowledged that the Most High God is sovereign over the kingdoms of men and sets over them anyone he wishes.
>
> "But you his son, O Belshazzar, have not humbled yourself, though you knew all this. Instead, you have set yourself up against the Lord of heaven. You had the goblets from his temple brought to you and you and your nobles, your wives and your concubines drank wine from them. You praised the gods of silver and gold, of bronze, iron, wood and stone, which cannot see or hear or understand. But you did not honor the God who holds in his hand your life and all your ways. Therefore he sent the hand that wrote the inscription."

Now Daniel, by the power God gave him, revealed the meaning of the message that was written on the wall and that filled King Belshazzar with fear.

> "This is the inscription that was written:
> MENE, MENE, TEKEL, PARSIN
> "This is what these words mean:
> *Mene*: God has numbered the days of your reign and brought it to an end.
> *Tekel*: You have been weighed on the scales and found wanting.
> *Peres*: Your kingdom is divided and given to the Medes and Persians."
>
> Then at Belshazzar's command, Daniel was clothed in purple, a gold chain was placed around his neck, and he was proclaimed the third highest ruler in the kingdom.
>
> That very night Belshazzar, king of the Babylonians, was slain, and Darius the Mede took over the kingdom, at the age of sixty-two. (Daniel 5:18–31)

Apparently, King Belshazzar wasn't too alarmed by the revelation. There was no attempt or desire on his part to repent, or even inquire why God was upset. We're told he gave Daniel the gold chain and made him the third highest ruler in Babylon, but there is no account of concern or anger about the proclamation that the kingdom was going to be given over to another nation. Perhaps the thought of the most powerful nation on earth being conquered seemed a little far-fetched. This, after all, was Babylon, the greatest nation on the face of the earth—There was no need to be concerned. But the consequences for ignoring the prophet's warning were disastrous.

That very night, a few hours after the frolicking party was shocked into stunned silence by the strange sight of a hand scribbling a phrase into the plaster wall, King Belshazzar was assassinated and the greatest kingdom on earth fell into the hands of Darius the Mede (a.k.a. Cyrus the Persian) in the year 539 BC.[3] A great kingdom was defeated, and a new kingdom rose in its place, as God prophesied would happen. God wasn't just aware it would happen; He caused it to happen because, as Daniel said, "… the Most High is sovereign over the kingdoms of men and gives them to anyone he wishes" (Daniel 4:17). Daniel had lived to see the head of gold replaced by the chest and arms of silver. For those who believe God, this is a loud, clear message against thinking any nation is impervious to collapse or defeat. No matter how great and powerful an army, no matter how far the reach of economic influence, no nation is beyond the plans of God.

Now as we look at Chapter 6, the final chapter on worship, we see the new leader, Darius, ruling over the Medo-Persian Empire. He had taken over the kingdom, killed King Belshazzar, and set up his government by appointing one hundred and twenty rulers over the whole kingdom and three administrators over the one hundred and twenty governors. He must have seen in Daniel what King Nebuchadnezzar saw, because he made Daniel one of the top three men in the kingdom. In fact, Daniel was so good at his job that King Darius planned to set him over the entire kingdom. How could this happen? How could one of the most trusted advisors of a former Babylonian king become a high-ranking official in the newly victorious Medo-Persian Empire? We can only speculate, but the way Babylon fell suggests there were many spies and subversives imbedded within the ranks of government, and they helped lead a coup of Belshazzar's power. Belshazzar was probably so absorbed in his hedonistic lifestyle he didn't realize plots were being devised against him. When Babylon fell, these spies most likely reported the remarkable wisdom and understanding of Daniel, especially the ability to predict the fall of Babylon and the rise of the Medes and Persians (in Chapter 5). There may even have been a person or two still around from King Nebuchadnezzar's days who personally knew Daniel's value as a trusted, wise counselor. What king wouldn't want to have an administrator like Daniel? Daniel, a member of the royal family of Israel/Judah, and formerly a top-ranking member in the kingdom of Babylon, became one of three administrators placed over the one hundred twenty rulers of the Medes and Persians. This is because of God's blessing of knowledge and understanding given to Daniel years ago. Daniel had impressed the king to the point that he was preparing to place Daniel over the whole kingdom. And this sets up the plot for one of the most famous events in the Bible.

> It pleased Darius to appoint 120 satraps to rule throughout the kingdom, with three administrators over them, one of whom was Daniel. The satraps were made accountable to them so that the king might not suffer loss. Now Daniel so distinguished himself among the administrators and the satraps by his exceptional qualities that the king planned to set him over the whole kingdom. At this, the administrators and the satraps tried to find grounds for charges against Daniel in his conduct of government affairs, but they were unable to do so. They could find no corruption in him, because he was trustworthy and neither corrupt nor negligent. Finally these men said, "We will never find any basis for charges against this man Daniel unless it has something to do with the law of his God.

Now imagine for a moment that you have been with Darius since his early days, or you became part of the plan for the coup d'etat in its infancy. Along comes this guy Daniel, who of all things is Jewish and was never part of the movement to put Darius on the throne, and the king is about to appoint him ruler over everyone. How could there not be some jealousy among the royal administrators and satraps? Daniel transcended changes in kings and nations—He always wound up on top. This, of course, is no mistake; God made sure Daniel was placed in these high positions, but the administrators and satraps set out to ruin Daniel and remove him from the top ranks of government.

> So the administrators and the satraps went as a group to the king and said: "O King Darius, live forever! The royal administrators, prefects, satraps, advisers and governors have all agreed that the king should issue an edict and enforce the decree that anyone who prays to any god or man during the next thirty days, except to you, O king, shall be thrown into the lions' den. Now, O king, issue the decree and put it in writing so that it cannot be altered—in accordance with the laws of the Medes and Persians, which cannot be repealed." So King Darius put the decree in writing. (Daniel 6:1–9)

This event is very similar to what happened to Shadrach, Meshach, and Abednego: An edict from the king was sent out commanding people to worship only the king. Daniel had the same choice his three friends had: Obey the king and live, or obey God and suffer death. But all four of these men chose to worship God without hesitation. They understood the extreme importance God placed on worshiping only Him. This is *not* something God overlooks or takes lightly or allows excuses for. When you know who God is, you worship *only* Him. This is still true today for the people of the new covenant.

So Daniel continued to pray to his God, even against the king's decree.

> Now when Daniel learned that the decree had been published, he went home to his upstairs room where the windows opened toward Jerusalem. Three times a day he got down on his knees and prayed, giving thanks to his God, just as he had done before.
>
> Then these men went as a group and found Daniel praying and asking God for help. So they went to the king and spoke to him about this royal decree: "Did you not publish a decree that during the next thirty days anyone who prays to any god or man except to you, O king, would be thrown into the lions' den?"
>
> The king answered, "The decree stands—in accordance with the laws of the Medes and Persians, which cannot be repealed." (Daniel 6:10–12)

The men then sprang the news on King Darius:

> Then they said to the king, "Daniel, who is one of the exiles from Judah, pays no attention to you, O king, or to the decree you put in writing. He still prays three times a day." When the king heard this, he was greatly distressed; he was determined to rescue Daniel and made every effort until sundown to save him. (Verses 13 and 14)

Unlike King Nebuchadnezzar who asked, "Then what god will be able to rescue you from my hand?" King Darius desperately searched for a way to save Daniel from his own decree. But even the king couldn't save Daniel: Once the king set a law, according to the Medes and Persians, it could not be revoked.

> Then the men went as a group to the king and said to him, "Remember, O king, that according to the law of the Medes and Persians no decree or edict that the king issues can be changed.
>
> So the king gave the order and they brought Daniel and threw him into the lions' den. The king said to Daniel, "May your God, whom you serve continually, rescue you!"
>
> A stone was brought and placed over the mouth of the den, and the king sealed it with his own signet ring and with the rings of his nobles, so that

Daniel's situation might not be changed. Then the king returned to his palace and spent the night without eating and without any entertainment being brought to him. And he could not sleep.

At the first light of dawn, the king got up and hurried to the lions' den. When he came near the den, he called to Daniel in an anguished voice, "Daniel, servant of the living God, has your God, whom you serve continually, been able to rescue you from the lions?" (Daniel 6:15–20)

King Darius liked Daniel and was about to entrust his kingdom to him before he was tricked into sending him to the lions. Unlike King Nebuchadnezzar, his attitude was one of hope—that Daniel's God might be able to rescue him from the king's hand.

Daniel answered, "O king, live forever! My God sent his angel, and he shut the mouths of the lions. They have not hurt me, because I was found innocent in his sight. Nor have I ever done any wrong before you, O king."

The king was overjoyed and gave orders to lift Daniel out of the den. And when Daniel was lifted from the den, no wound was found on him, because he had trusted in his God.

The king was thrilled Daniel was unharmed; there wasn't a bite or scratch found on him. He had spent a night in a den of ravenous lions—but God intervened. Instead, the instigators of this plot, and their families, received the punishment they tried to impose on Daniel.

At the king's command, the men who had falsely accused Daniel were brought in and thrown into the lions' den, along with their wives and children. And before they reached the floor of the den, the lions overpowered them and crushed all their bones.

Then King Darius wrote to all the peoples, nations and men of every language throughout the land:

"May you prosper greatly!

"I issue a decree that in every part of my kingdom people must fear and reverence the God of Daniel.

"For he is the living God and he endures forever; his kingdom will not be destroyed, his dominion will never end. He rescues and he saves; he performs signs and wonders in the heavens and on the earth. He has rescued Daniel from the power of the lions."

So Daniel prospered during the reign of Darius and the reign of Cyrus the Persian. (Daniel 6:21–28)

The decree Darius sent to every part of his kingdom is pretty amazing. Remember what the men told the king: "Remember, O king, that according to the law of the Medes and Persians no decree or edict that the king issues can be changed." This went for the new decree as well.

It's also amazing to see how much Darius knew about God—He endures forever, and his kingdom will endure forever, never to be destroyed. How could he have understood the power of the Living God? Although Darius saw how God worked miraculously to rescue Daniel from the lions, I think it involved more than that. I believe Darius and Daniel spent many hours talking about God, His promise to Abraham, and the dream revealed to King Nebuchadnezzar about future kingdoms. Darius was probably amazed and intrigued by all of the things Daniel revealed to him, and perhaps that's why the king was so disheartened when Daniel was sentenced to death in the lions' den. Daniel, as it turns out, was a pretty good witness to Gentile kings. As God said many times, Gentile kings and their people were often more receptive to God's message and miracles than were the people of Israel, whom God called "stiff-necked."

After being rescued, the Bible tells us Daniel prospered. He was most likely appointed overseer of the whole kingdom, just as he had been during the reign of King Nebuchadnezzar.

As we close out this chapter on the importance of worshiping the true God, it's worth thinking about what God says in Chapters 1, 3, 4, 5, and 6 of Daniel. Each miraculous event highlights the fact that when you know who God is, you worship *only Him*—even under the threat of death. Jesus Christ says in Matthew 16: "If anyone would come after me, he must deny himself and take up his cross and follow me. For whoever wants to save his life will lose it, but whoever loses his life for me will find it. What good will it be for a man if he gains the whole world, yet forfeits his soul? Or what can a man give in exchange for his soul?" (verses 24–26). God says there is nothing that should be chosen above worshiping Him—not even saving your own life. God is able to save us from *anything*, but we are to worship Him whether He protects us from death or not. He takes worship seriously. Worshiping other gods for any reason goes completely against His commands. We are also reminded that God controls the destiny of nations and their rulers. When kings who knew better failed to worship God, they were removed from power—temporarily or permanently. God is sovereign over all.

Both Nebuchadnezzar and Darius write about the kingdom of God, which in a sense makes them the first to preach the Gospel to Gentiles—six hundred years before the apostle Paul does the same thing. The two kings believed in the God of Israel, His power, and His everlasting kingdom through the miracles they experienced. You might say, "With those miraculous events, who wouldn't believe and obey?!" But remember when Jesus Christ—God in the flesh—came down to live on earth and performed incredible miracles, few believed His message about His power and coming kingdom even though He exhorted them to believe in the miracles.

With the idea of worshiping the Living God in mind, I think a proper end to this chapter is found in the book of Deuteronomy, Chapter 6 where we read the very commands God gave Israel over 3,500 years ago—commands they failed to follow and that caused them to be destroyed and scattered:

> Hear O Israel: The Lord our God, the Lord is one. Love the Lord your God with all your heart and with all your soul and with all your strength. These commandments that I give you today are to be upon your hearts. Impress them on your children. Talk about them when you sit at home and when you walk along the road, when you lie down and when you get up. Tie them as symbols on your hands and bind them on your foreheads. Write them on the doorframes of your houses and your gates.
>
> When the Lord your God brings you into the land he swore to your fathers, to Abraham, Isaac and Jacob, to give you—a land with large flourishing cities you did not build, houses filled with all kinds of good things you did not provide, wells you did not dig, and vineyards and olive groves you did not plant—then when you eat and are satisfied, be careful that you do not forget the Lord who brought you out of Egypt, out of the land of slavery.
>
> Fear the Lord your God, serve him only and take your oaths in his name. Do not follow other gods, the gods of the peoples around you; for the Lord your God, who is among you, is a jealous God and his anger will burn against you, and he will destroy you from the face of the land." (Deuteronomy 6: 4–15)

God takes worship—obedience to Him—seriously. Because one man, Abraham, worshiped God, God promised to bless all the nations of the earth through him. That's the hope of the final, everlasting kingdom that Kings Nebuchadnezzar and Darius spoke about.

How great is God! He blesses with love and forgiveness. He searches the innermost thoughts—Nothing is beyond His understanding. Despite man's sinful ways, God promises to wipe away our tears and remove death forever. And because of His love He sent His only son to this earth to die, and He resurrected Him from death so that we too may live forever with Him in His eternal kingdom. Our God is a great and loving God! How could we not worship Him the way He wants us to worship Him? There is no other God like this!

6

The Compass of Prophecy: Daniel's Prayer and the Coming Messiah

Daniel Chapter 9 is like no other chapter in the book; it isn't a standoff between people worshiping idols and people worshiping God, and it isn't a chapter prophesying kingdoms from Daniel's time until the end when God sets up His kingdom. Instead, the first two-thirds of this chapter records a beautiful, sincere prayer of repentance and praise in which Daniel asks forgiveness for himself and his people and then goes on to ask God to restore Jerusalem and the sanctuary, the hope of all Israelites in exile. In the last part of the chapter, there is the most specific—and difficult to understand—prophecy found in the Bible describing the arrival of Jesus Christ. This prophecy, which is most commonly called "the seventy 'sevens,'" not only pinpoints the arrival of the Messiah; it still has relevant meaning in international events now. As we explore this chapter, we will see more of the relationship between God and Daniel, we'll look at an all-encompassing prayer about Israel, we'll try to unravel an incredibly complex prophecy that few understood even when it was fulfilled, and we'll see what has yet to be fulfilled.

Chapter 9 is written in the first year of Darius the Medes' rule over the Medo-Persian kingdom. Daniel says, "I, Daniel, understood from the Scriptures, according to the word of the Lord given to Jeremiah the prophet, that the desolation of Jerusalem would last seventy years. So I turned to the Lord God and pleaded with him in prayer and petition, in fasting, and in sackcloth and ashes." Why did understanding of the scriptures cause such consternation for Daniel? Because he knew there was a problem. Daniel was a man who followed the Law of Moses so he knew the law required animal sacrifices to be offered for personal and national sin, and the sacrifices could not be offered anywhere except the temple of the Lord on Mount Moriah, where God had placed His name.

The temple wasn't just a place where offerings were made; it was where God dwelt among His people, where He placed His name. Essentially, God's physical address on earth was the Holy of Holies on Mount Moriah in Jerusalem. Long ago, King David had purchased the temple land when God instructed him to buy the threshing floor of Araunah the Jebusite (II Samuel 24:18–21), and David's son, King Solomon, built the temple on that land (II Chronicles 3:1). Solomon's temple (the first temple) had the ark of the Lord's covenant and two cherubim overlaid with gold inside the Most Holy Place. When the temple was finished and the ark was placed inside, "The trumpeters and singers joined in unison, as with one voice, to give praise and thanks to the Lord. Accompanied by trumpets, cymbals and other instruments, they raised their voices in praise to the Lord and sang: 'He is good; his love endures forever.' Then the temple of the Lord was filled with a cloud, and the priests could not perform their service because of the cloud, for the glory of the Lord filled the temple of God" (II Chronicles 5:13, 14).

Every day, morning and evening sacrifices were offered to God, and every holy day or festival—there were seven—was centered on the temple. The importance of the temple is especially clear on the Day of Atonement, a day where the nation of Israel fasted and made atonement for their sins. There was one room in the temple that was only used on this day. This room, called the inner sanctuary, or the Most Holy Place, or the Holy of Holies, was where "the ark of the Lord's covenant" resided. The only man who could enter this room was the high priest, and it was here he sprinkled the blood from the sacrifice for his sins so he could then sprinkle the blood from the sacrifice for the sins of the nation. This was how the nation of Israel restored their relationship with God every year. If anyone else at any other time went into this room, they would instantly die. But the temple had been destroyed in 586 BC when the Babylonians sacked Jerusalem. That caused a great problem for Daniel and other Israelites keeping the law: Without the temple, there could be no offering for sin, and if there was no offering for sin, there was no forgiveness of sin, and in a sinful state, there was no relationship with God. In fact, without the temple, the Law of Moses was essentially defunct, because the whole law was centered on God's people offering sacrifices to pay the penalty of sin.

Daniel realized he would most likely be dead by the time Jerusalem was reclaimed. He'd die without being able to atone for his sins; he would die in sin, a total anathema to a law keeper from the house of Judah. This was extremely discouraging to Daniel and thus sets the tone for verse three. "So I turned to the Lord God and pleaded with him in prayer and petition, in fasting, and in sackcloth and ashes." Daniel was so concerned about this situation that he asked God to intervene to change or speed up the prophecy of Jeremiah. How incredible! To Daniel, being at one with God was tantamount to life itself. This attitude was quite different from the prevailing sentiment among some of the Israelites when Jesus Christ came to the world for the forgiveness of sins hundreds of years later. At that time, some people dismissed his ministry because they wanted a *nationalistic* savior, someone to restore the nation of Israel back to the glory days of David and Solomon, not a savior from sin. But to God, the forgiveness of sin is more important than any nation or nationalistic pride, because unforgiven sin acts as a block in the relationship between God and human beings; it's an unpaid debt that is outstanding. The debt has to be paid or there is a default, and if there is a default—or non-forgiveness of your sins—when you die, what does that mean? Well, a faithful, law-keeping Israelite would know that if you died in your sins, it threw into question what would happen to you personally at the resurrection on the Last Great Day. We will discuss this more when the subject, and Daniel's answer from God, presents itself later on in Chapters 11 and 12. But suffice it to say, this was on Daniel's mind as he prayed to God.

So Daniel prayed and confessed to God:

> "O Lord, the great and awesome God who keeps his covenant of love with all who love him and obey his commands, we have sinned and done wrong. We have been wicked and have rebelled; we have turned away from your commands and laws. We have not listened to your servants the prophets, who spoke in your name to our kings, our princes and our fathers, and to all the people of the land.
>
> Lord, you are righteous, but this day we are covered in shame—the men of Judah and people of Jerusalem and all Israel, both near and far, in all the countries where you have scattered us because of our unfaithfulness to you. O Lord, we and our kings, our princes and our fathers are covered with shame because we have sinned against you. The Lord our God is merciful and forgiving, even though we have rebelled against him; we have not obeyed the Lord our God or kept the laws he gave us through his servants the prophets. All Israel has transgressed your law and turned away refusing to obey you."
> (Daniel 9:11)

Daniel pleads "guilty" to Israel's unfaithfulness to God because he's fully aware of all that went wrong in the six hundred or so years of Israel's existence. He also acknowledges the great love, mercy, and patience God showed by warning them again and again through the prophets even though Israel continued to run after other gods. Daniel describes Israel as being covered in shame, meaning her people's sin had not been blotted out—It stood as a symbol for all to see that they were not clean but instead covered in filth: Israel was in a state of disgrace.

Now for the consequences:

> "Therefore the curses and sworn judgments written in the Law of Moses, the servant of God, have been poured out on us, because we have sinned against you. You have fulfilled the words spoken against us and our rulers by bringing upon us great disaster. Under the whole heaven nothing has ever been done like what has been done to Jerusalem. Just as it is written in the Law of Moses, all of this disaster has come upon us, yet we have not sought the favor of the Lord our God by turning from our sins and giving attention to your truth. The Lord did not hesitate to bring the disaster upon us, for the Lord our God is righteous in everything he does; yet we have not obeyed him." (Daniel 9:11–14)

Here Daniel refers to Chapter 28 in the book of Deuteronomy, where God promises blessings and curses according to Israel's faithfulness. Blessings of abundance and prosperity are promised if Israel obeys God and follows the covenant they made with Him, and curses of disease, decline, and ultimately destruction if they disobey God and break the covenant. As we previously said, God takes promises and oaths seriously. He expected Israel to do what they said they would, because, as Daniel points out, God did what He said He would do: He blessed them when they obeyed His covenant and brought curses when they disobeyed His covenant. Daniel acknowledged that God was right to bring disaster upon Israel because of their disobedience; furthermore, whatever God does is righteous because He is God over all.

Now Daniel begins to make his request:

> "Now, O Lord our God, who brought your people out of Egypt with a mighty hand and who made for yourself a name that endures to this day, we have sinned, we have done wrong. O Lord, in keeping with all your righteous acts, turn away your anger and your wrath from Jerusalem, your city, your holy hill. Our sins and the iniquities of our fathers have made Jerusalem and your people an object of scorn to all those around us."

Daniel states that God has done great wonders, but it's the behavior of the people that has caused the disaster brought upon Israel. However, Daniel pleads with God on behalf of His nameHis name on His city Jerusalem and His name on His temple mount—to turn away His anger, despite the behavior of the people. He continues:

"Now, our God, hear the prayers and petitions of your servant. For your sake, O Lord, look with favor on your desolate sanctuary. Give ear, O God, and hear; open your eyes and see the desolation of the city that bears your Name. We do not make requests of you because we are righteous, but because of your great mercy. O Lord, listen! O Lord, forgive! O Lord, hear and act! For your sake, O my God, do not delay, because your city and your people bear your Name."

While I was speaking and praying, confessing my sin and the sin of my people Israel and making my request to the Lord my God for his holy hill—while I was still in prayer, Gabriel, the man I had seen in the earlier vision, came to me in swift flight about the time of the evening sacrifice.

Daniel here lets us know the purpose of his prayer. The whole summation of this prayer is the confession of his sins and all of Israel's sins so that God will reestablish the place where sacrifice can be performed and sins forgiven. Daniel knows that can only come when the "holy hill" is restored in Jerusalem. The ability for God's people to pray and simply ask for forgiveness without animal sacrifice is still about six hundred years away when the new covenant is established through the sacrifice of Jesus Christ. Under this new covenant, we are told in the book of Hebrews that because of Christ, God's people can walk with confidence into the Holy of Holies "in full assurance of faith having our hearts sprinkled to cleanse us from a guilty conscience and having our bodies washed with pure water" (Hebrews 10:22). But Daniel is still under the old covenant. So in Daniel's mind, without restoration of the temple, there can be no forgiveness. But during Daniel's prayer, something unusual happens. He hasn't even finished his request when the angel Gabriel interrupts him! God immediately sends an answer about sin and his holy hill. "While I was still in prayer, Gabriel, the man I had seen in the earlier vision, came to me in swift flight about the time of the evening sacrifice" (9:21). I don't believe it's a coincidence that Daniel's prayer coincides with the evening sacrifice. When the temple existed, there was always an evening and morning sacrifice along with other offerings, and most people probably prayed when the daily sacrifices were being offered. It was probably Daniel's custom to pray during this time. Daniel also mentions that he had seen Gabriel in an earlier vision, referring to the vision of Chapter 8. Interestingly, that vision is called the "vision of the evenings and mornings", referring to the sacrifices.

Daniel says that Gabriel came to instruct him. In verse 22, Gabriel says, "Daniel, I have now come to give you insight and understanding. As soon as you began to pray, an answer was given, which I have come to tell you, for you are highly esteemed." Why would God send a message to Daniel telling him he was highly esteemed? Because Daniel was extremely unsettled by the fact that he could not offer sacrifices for the forgiveness of his sins and the sins of his nation. Daniel knew he and his people were covered in sin. In his prayer, and in his heart, Daniel knew the sins of Israel were the reason Jerusalem and the temple were desolate and his people were scattered as exiles in Persia and elsewhere. However, God thought so much of Daniel's disposition that He sent an angel immediately to tell him that he, Daniel, was highly esteemed in God's sight. Because of his faithfulness to God, God thought very highly of Daniel and told him of future events that hadn't been revealed to anyone else in the Old Testament.

What is about to follow is one of the greatest prophecies in the entire Bible. We have looked at many incredible prophecies so far, but this next prophecy is very different because it involves a matter that is most important to God—the forgiveness of sin! But the fulfillment of this prophecy was completely missed by the majority of people 2,000 or so years ago. People like to delve into exciting prophecies to find out what nations will rule when, or when the "Antichrist" will arrive, or when Jesus Christ will arrive. Atoning for sin apparently isn't as sensational; however, to Daniel, it was very important, and that's why Gabriel tells Daniel he has an answer to his prayer.

Daniel is told at the end of verse 23 to "consider the message and understand the vision." As we begin to go through the prophecy, it's important to remember Daniel was requesting that God restore His holy temple so there could be atonement for the sins of Israel. That's the key to understanding this prophecy.

> "Seventy "sevens" are decreed for your people and your holy city to finish transgression, to put an end to sin, to atone for wickedness, to bring in everlasting righteousness, to seal up vision and prophecy and to anoint the most holy." (Daniel 9:24)

The belief here is that each "seven" is seven years, and there will be "seventy" of those seven-year time periods, for a total of 490 years. Remember, all of this started off with Daniel stating he knew that according to Jeremiah the prophet, Jerusalem's desolation would last seventy years, and thus Daniel believed all would be well after the seventy years were over. However, what God is saying here is that the plan involves not seventy years, but 490 years. This prophecy doesn't nullify Jeremiah's prophecy because a restoration occurred in 516 BC, seventy years after the temple was destroyed in 586 BC. But this "seventy 'sevens'" prophecy involved something more than just the occupation of a city and the hope of a restored physical temple building. The list of events that would be accomplished in 490 years is amazing: Daniel's people and Jerusalem finish a time of transgression, an end is put to sin, atonement is made for wickedness, everlasting righteousness is brought in, vision and prophecy are sealed up, and the Most Holy One or Most Holy Place is anointed. What does this list mean? Everything points to God sending an "end"—atonement—for sin and establishing a new system and a new temple. The new temple, the place where the offering for sin is made, is going to be very different than what Daniel is asking for.

This prophecy describes the work of the Messiah, the reason He would be coming in 490 years: A period of time had been decreed by God for the transgressions of Israel and Jerusalem to be finished, and with the Messiah comes an end to sin, wickedness, and the bringing of everlasting righteousness. But what could "sealing up vision and prophecy" possibly mean? Well, here is a thought to consider: The office of prophet would officially end with Jesus Christ; He was the last one considered to be God's direct connection to the people, or the nation of Israel. However, prophecy itself would continue because many were able to prophesy through the power of the Spirit after the Pentecost in AD 31. But understanding of prophecy was limited only to those with the Spirit. Remember when the disciples asked Christ why He spoke in parables in Luke 8:10. He answered, "The knowledge of the secrets of the kingdom of God has been given to you, but to others I speak in parables, so that, 'though seeing, they may not see; though hearing, they may not understand.'" This scripture is most likely talking about restricting seeing and hearing to only those whom God calls, not the entire nation.

The rest of the chapter describes events that were to occur.

> "Know and understand this: From the issuing of the decree to restore and rebuild Jerusalem until the Anointed One, the ruler, comes, there will be seven 'sevens,' and sixty-two 'sevens.'"

So Gabriel tells Daniel that from the issuing of the decree until the arrival of the Messiah, there will be forty-nine years (seven 'sevens') plus 434 years (sixty-two 'sevens'), or 483 years total. Because there were many decrees to restore and rebuild Jerusalem, it's difficult to know what date to use to start counting 483 years. Cyrus of Persia issued the first decree in 539 BC. At that time, some Israelites went back to Jerusalem with Zerubbabel to rebuild the temple. There was some opposition from the local people that caused the construction to be delayed for eighteen years until 521 BC. In 521 BC, Darius, king of Persia, issued a second decree to let the people finish construction of the temple, and in 515 BC, the temple was finished and ready to be used for offerings and sacrifice (see the introduction to the book of Ezra in Zondervan's NIV). This completion of the temple occurred exactly seventy years after Jerusalem was sacked and destroyed by King Nebuchadnezzar, which completes the prophecy given to Jeremiah: "I will banish them from the sounds of joy and gladness, the voices of bride and bridegroom, the sound of millstones and the light of the lamp. This whole country will become a desolate wasteland, and these nations will serve the king of Babylon seventy years" (Jeremiah 25:11). This is the very prophecy Daniel has in mind as he begins his prayer. How should we use these decrees when computing the arrival of the Messiah? We have the advantage of looking back on history, and we know if we use any of the above "decree" dates and add 483 years, we don't land at the time of Christ. For example, 539 BC plus 483 years puts us at 56 BC where there is a lot of activity in Rome, but nothing to do with the Anointed One, Jesus Christ.

But there was another decree issued by King Artaxerxes of Persia in 458 BC in which Ezra came to Jerusalem to restore not just the temple, but also the city and the former ways of life, even restoring the offices of priest, judge, and magistrate. These people were to govern the area much like the days of old. All of this information can be found in the book of Ezra. The key to the prophecy is that the city of Jerusalem will be restored and rebuilt. What took place under Ezra around 458 BC is more akin to this prophecy than what took place in 515 BC. The *exact* date for Ezra's return is somewhat controversial[4] and may be off by a year or so, but what's important is this date leaves us at the time of Christ. If we take the date 456 BC and add 483 years, we come out to AD 27, which is around the time Jesus Christ was baptized, or anointed, and began His ministry. It is important to realize the *birth* of Christ is not being prophesied here. Jesus's birth, although important, is not an anointing, and the prophecy talks specifically about the Anointed One. Additionally, the Bible spends very little time on Jesus's life prior to baptism. It's after the baptism—the anointing that begins His ministry—that the Bible really starts to chronicle the activities and events of Jesus Christ's life, death, and resurrection. Of the eighty-nine chapters in the four gospels, only four chapters talk about the birth of Christ. The other eighty-five chapters chronicle the events of His ministry and death.

The arrival of "the Anointed One, the ruler" takes place in Matthew 3:13–17 when Jesus Christ is baptized and officially begins His ministry on earth around AD 27. Jerusalem had been rebuilt, but the area was under Roman rule and the Jews chafed at the occupation. At the end of Jesus Christ's ministry, He is "cut off" (verse 26), crucified at twilight on Passover, AD 31. This is what is meant when it says, "Seventy 'sevens' are decreed for your people and your city … to put an end to sin" in verse 24. Although people continue to sin, the penalty—eternal death—has been ended, and now Jesus Christ holds the keys to death. Revelation 1:18 says, "I am the Living One; I was dead, and behold I am alive for ever and ever! And I hold the keys of death and Hades."

This is a good place to look at why Jesus Christ died. There are many in the Christian community who blame the Jews for killing Christ, fueling anti-Semitic feelings and actions. But Christ's death was the whole purpose for His short time on earth. In Matthew 16:21–23, it says,

> From that time on, Jesus began to explain to his disciples that he must go to Jerusalem and suffer many things at the hands of the elders, chief priests and teachers of the law, and that he must be killed and on the third day be raised to life.
> Peter took him aside and began to rebuke him. "Never, Lord!" he said. "This shall never happen to you!"
> Jesus turned and said to Peter, "Get behind me, Satan! You are a stumbling block to me; you do not have in mind the things of God, but the things of men."

God's plan was to have Jesus Christ die on a specific day, at a specific time, in a specific way. He had prophesied it throughout the Old Testament, and the prophecies were going to be fulfilled. We see that John the Baptist understood this when he saw Christ and said, "Look, the Lamb of God, who takes away the sin of the world!" In I Corinthians 5:7, Paul also understood this when he said, "For Christ, our Passover lamb, has been sacrificed." The Israelites, while they were slaves in Egypt, were told by God to choose a lamb, slaughter it, and wipe the blood on the doorposts as a sign to the Lord to pass over their houses. This was symbolic of what was to come. The real event being pictured was the sacrifice of the Lamb of God who covered us with His blood and allowed eternal death to pass over us. When you understand this, it doesn't make sense to blame anyone for killing Christ. God ordained that He would die, even down to the time and events. As Peter learned, anyone who tried to stop what God ordained was doing the work of Satan.

And why did Jesus Christ have to die? Most Christians are already familiar with the passage in John 3:16–18, "For God so loved the world that he gave his one and only Son, that whoever believes in him shall not perish but have eternal life. For God did not send his Son into the world to condemn the world, but to save the world through him. Whoever believes in him is not condemned, but whoever does not believe stands condemned already because he has not believed in the name of God's one and only Son."

Romans 6:22, 23 says, "But now that you have been set free from sin and have become slaves to God, the benefit you reap leads to holiness, and the result is eternal life. For the wages of sin is death, but the gift of God is eternal life in Christ Jesus our Lord." This was always the plan, that Jesus would give His life to pay the debt we brought on ourselves by disobeying God—sinning—and therefore allow us to be saved from eternal death by giving us eternal life. Christ's death was imminent because of the first action of disobedience to God in the Garden of Eden. God told Adam and Eve, "You are free to eat from any tree in the garden; but you must not eat from the tree of the knowledge of good and evil, for when you eat of it you will surely die" (Genesis 2:16, 17). Satan lied and told Adam he wouldn't die; mankind has continued to live under Satan and follow him by disobeying God and bringing on the penalty of eternal death. So much more could be said, but that's for another book. Suffice it to say that at this point, man was doomed to death *forever*, eternal death. However, God made a promise to Abraham to "bless all nations on earth" through his offspring, and He swore by Himself that this would be accomplished even if it meant that God would have to come down and pay the penalty for sin Himself, which of course He did. Because of Christ's sacrifice and resurrection, mankind can be resurrected from death and given eternal life. So we now see why "the Anointed One will be cut off" and how that will "put an end to sin." The penalty of sin—death—is now paid for the whole world.

There is an interesting side note to this prophecy that Daniel's been given. There's a connection between Daniel and the birth of the above-mentioned Anointed One. As we know, Daniel is in charge of all the "wise men" in Persia at the time he receives the prophecy of the seventy "sevens." He had also been in charge of the same in Babylon and had even saved them from death. They all knew Daniel had a very special connection to God; they had seen miracles performed that they themselves could not understand, and they had all seen and heard Nebuchadnezzar and Cyrus proclaim great and wonderful praise to Daniel's God. This is just speculation, but I believe Daniel talked with some of his charges, and maybe the kings, about the coming events revealed in this prophecy. In the prophecy, the "Anointed One" is called a ruler, or king, so when Christ was born, it was understood that a king was being born, and "Christ" and "Messiah" both mean "the Anointed One." Some of the wise men were astrologers as we learned back in Chapter 2, and they looked to the stars for answers, especially when predicting the future. Interestingly, God used a star five and a half centuries later to bring wise men, or magi, from the east to the exact location of the newly born Christ in Bethlehem. "After Jesus was born in Bethlehem in Judea, during the time of King Herod, Magi from the east [Persia, Media, and Babylon?] came to Jerusalem and asked, "Where is the one who has been born king of the Jews? We saw his star in the east and have come to worship him" (Matthew 2:1, 2). Why would magi, or wise men, travel all the way to Judea to see the baby Jesus as recorded in the Gospel of Matthew? Could it be they knew of this prophecy, and God made it so their descendants 550 years later would see the prophecy fulfilled? The wise men searched for the "king of the Jews" because Daniel was Jewish and the prophecy involves his people and his city. It only stands to reason that they'd be searching for a king of the Jews. When the wise men found Jesus, "they bowed down and worshiped him. Then they opened their treasures and presented Him with gifts of gold and of incense and of myrrh" (Matthew 2:11). The gift of gold was given because Jesus was a king; the incense and myrrh are used for anointing and embalming—two important events coming in Christ's life. The wise men were part of a handful of people who knew who this baby really was. Imagine! They bowed to and worshiped Jesus Christ. Few people did that in Christ's entire lifetime. But the magi knew this was a king. Afterward, God, through a dream, told the wise men not to go back and tell Herod where Jesus was. This wasn't strange or unusual to them; several times in the book of Daniel, we see they are called on to interpret dreams—a common event for them in their line of work. I don't think it's too much of a stretch to say that the visit of the magi was directly related to the prophecy of the seventy "sevens." Because of all that was written, they believed what was said in the prophecy and treated the Anointed One accordingly.

There is one more thing to note from this passage before we move on. The Anointed One, Jesus Christ, is referred to as "the ruler." He is the *only one* in this chapter referred to as "the ruler." This will be important to remember when we read verse 26.

Starting the prophecy again right before verse 26:

> It will be rebuilt with streets and a trench, but in times of trouble. After the sixty-two "sevens," the Anointed One will be cut off and will have nothing [or "no one"]. The people of the ruler who will come will destroy the city and the sanctuary. The end will come like a flood: War will continue until the end, and desolations have been decreed.

By the time Ezra arrived in 558 BC, and later Nehemiah in 444 BC, Jerusalem's walls and infrastructure were in the process of being rebuilt, which again makes 456 BC the better starting date for the 483 years (seven "sevens" and sixty-two "sevens"). Prior to this time, Jerusalem's wall, or defense, had still been in shambles from the plunder of Nebuchadnezzar in 586 BC. In the book of Nehemiah 2:17, Nehemiah talks about the wall, "Then I said to them, 'You see the trouble we are in: Jerusalem lies in ruins, and its gates have been burned with fire. Come, let us rebuild the wall of Jerusalem, and we will no longer be in disgrace.'" And so Nehemiah went about repairing the wall and the gates of Jerusalem, but not the temple since it had essentially been rebuilt seventy-one or so years earlier.

Nehemiah also notes the "trouble" that occurred as the rebuilding went on: "But when Sanballat, Tobiah, the Arabs, the Ammonites and the men of Ashdod heard that the repairs to Jerusalem's walls had gone ahead and that the gaps were being closed, they were very angry. They all plotted together to come and fight against Jerusalem and stir up trouble against it. But we prayed to our God and posted a guard day and night to meet this threat" (Nehemiah 4:7–9). There is even further trouble chronicled in Chapter 6.

More importantly, after 586, Jerusalem is under the control of Gentile kings, so that up to the time of Christ, Jerusalem remained a subjugated, and sometimes persecuted, city. When Christ walked the streets of Jerusalem, it was the Romans who were in control, and Jerusalem stayed under foreign (non-Jewish) control all the way up to 1967. We'll talk more about that event when we cover Chapter 11.

We are told that after the 483 years, the "Anointed One" will be cut off and have no one. We know of course that Jesus Christ was "cut off," crucified, in AD 31, and we also know He died alone; His followers were scattered, and even Peter denied knowing Him. Christ foretold this in Mark 14:27: "'You will all fall away,' Jesus told them, 'for it is written: "I will strike the shepherd, and the sheep will be scattered."'" At the time of His death, which occurred on Passover, it seemed the movement He had led was dead. What was the movement all about anyway? What was expected of Him? The Jewish people expected a savior to bring back the free and independent nation of Israel, just like it was in the days of David and Solomon. When Jesus talked about the kingdom of God, the people were thinking, *A free and independent nation right now!* The Jewish people were tired of being oppressed by foreign rulers. Their hope was in a national savior, but as we shall read, that was not the mission of this king, or the request made by Daniel earlier in this chapter. As we read in the book of John 18:37, Christ proclaimed that He was, in fact, a king:

"You are a king, then!" said Pilate.

Jesus answered, "You are right in saying I am a king. In fact, for this reason I was born, and for this I came into the world, to testify to the truth. Everyone on the side of truth listens to me."

The original question by Pilate in verse 33 was, "Are you the king of the Jews?" or in other words, "Are you the ruler of the people?" The Anointed One and the ruler, as noted back in verse 25 of Daniel, are one and the same. When the term "the ruler" is mentioned here, it applies only to Jesus Christ.

This prophecy of the seventy "sevens" was announcing a great event that was going to happen: a new temple was coming, one that would be indestructible, accessible to *all*, and a place where sin was truly forgiven. God was telling Daniel it would take 490 years for this new temple to be in place. That new temple is mentioned in the book of John, where Jesus Christ says,

"Destroy this temple, and I will raise it again in three days."

The Jews replied, "It has taken forty-six years to build this temple, and you are going to raise it in three days?" But the temple he had spoken of was his body. After he was raised from the dead, his disciples recalled what he had said. Then they believed the Scripture and the words that Jesus had spoken." (John 2:19–22)

The new temple is Jesus Christ, where God placed His name and where one offering has been made for the forgiveness of all sins. The apostle Paul says that all the animal sacrifices offered in the old covenant never really forgave sin; they just pointed to the sacrifice that ultimately would—Jesus Christ. If the animal sacrifices had really paid the penalty for sin, why would Christ have had to come at all? God wanted Israel to understand the concept of sacrifice and therefore instituted a temporary covenant until a better one was in place. This coming temple doesn't diminish the geographic significance of the original temple on Mount Moriah. We know through the gospels that Christ spent a good deal of time there, and He called the temple built by Herod His "father's house," meaning it was still a place God recognized as His and where He accepted offerings and sacrifices because the old covenant was still in effect at that time. So the definition of the temple is the place where God places His name, or dwells, and where sin is forgiven.

The next part of the prophecy in verse 26 is somewhat controversial. It says, "The people of the ruler who will come will destroy the city and the sanctuary." The "people" mentioned here are the Jewish people, not the Romans, because the ruler in this prophecy is Jesus Christ. When the Roman general Titus brought his six-month siege against Jerusalem, many internecine squabbles between Jewish factions resulted in the destruction of many parts of the city, and instead of uniting as one force, they fought against each other as the Romans watched from the hills. And it was the Jews, not the Romans, who first set fire to the temple; the Romans ultimately finished the task and completely destroyed the temple. The Jewish people had a hand in the destruction of the city, and it was a rebellion that they had led that caused its ultimate downfall.[5]

Verse 26 continues, "The end will come like a flood: War will continue until the end, and desolations have been decreed." Here Daniel is told that conflict around Jerusalem would continue until the end of the age. After the destruction of Jerusalem in AD 70, and again in AD 135, there was nothing left of Jerusalem but a heap of rubble. Its walls, homes, and temple all lay in ruin, just as if a flood had occurred. Subsequently after both destructions, "abominations"—altars to *other* gods—were set up on the holy hill of Mount Moriah. In AD 135, the temple of Jupiter was set up and ultimately the Dome of the Rock in 691, that still stands to this very day. From what we see, it seems that desolations will stay in effect until the end of the age and the return of Jesus Christ. There are those who are waiting for a rebuilding of the temple on Mount Moriah so that sacrifices can once again be offered. However, the next verse explains why this may not occur and desolations will stay in effect until the return of Jesus Christ.

Before looking at verse 27, it's important to remember two things: First, the "he" we are going to talk about is the "Anointed One" *and* the "ruler" referred to earlier in the passage, because the entire prophecy is about that same person. Gabriel didn't suddenly start talking about someone else—an end-time ruler, as some believe. Instead, he continued to talk about Jesus Christ. Second, this is the seventieth "seven" being discussed, and the focus of this seven-year period is Christ's ministry. Remember that seventy "sevens" are decreed and seven "sevens" and sixty-two "sevens" have already been discussed. These "sevens" occur chronologically, or in a row. The seventieth "seven" began when Jesus Christ was anointed and started His ministry. Some people believe instead that 483 years went by, then Christ arrived, then thousands of years transpire to bring about an end-time beast power, and then the events of the last "seven" occur. This isn't the case. Verse 27 continues the discussion about Jesus Christ—the Anointed One:

> He will confirm a covenant with many for one "seven." In the middle of the "seven" he will put an end to sacrifice and offering. And one who causes deso-

lation will come upon the pinnacle of the abominable temple, until the end that is decreed is poured out on the desolated city. [See footnote in NIV.]

So let's look at what is happening in this last "seven." The Anointed One makes a covenant with many as recorded in Luke 22:20: "In the same way, after the supper he took the cup, saying, 'This cup is the new covenant in my blood, which is poured out for you.'" Christ's ministry lasts three and a half years and ends with Him sacrificing His life "in the middle of the 'seven.'" It's at this time that He puts an end to sacrifice and offering. The animal sacrifices and offerings of the old covenant were symbolic of this very event. It was extremely difficult for many who were Jewish to accept this new system—even in the New Testament church! Many of the New Testament letters written by the apostles to the Jews in the church spend time explaining that the old system wasn't meant to be permanent. Instead, that system was meant to carry the Israelites until the *real* sacrifice occurred, and now ALL nations would be blessed through Abraham's seed. Chapter 9 of the book of Hebrews puts it this way:

> But [under the old covenant] only the high priest entered the inner room, and that only once a year, and never without blood, which he offered for himself and for the sins the people had committed in ignorance. The Holy Spirit was showing by this that the way into the Most Holy Place had not yet been disclosed as long as the first tabernacle was still standing. This is an illustration for the present time, indicating that the gifts and sacrifices being offered were not able to clear the conscience of the worshiper. They are only a matter of food and drink and various ceremonial washings—external regulations applying until the time of the new order.
>
> When Christ came as high priest of the good things that are already here, he went through the greater and more perfect tabernacle that is not manmade, that is to say, not a part of this creation. He did not enter by means of the blood of goats and calves; but he entered the Most Holy Place once for all by his own blood, having obtained eternal redemption. The blood of goats and bulls and the ashes of a heifer sprinkled on those who are ceremonially unclean sanctify them so that they are outwardly clean. How much more, then, will the blood of Christ, who through the eternal Spirit offered himself unblemished to God, cleanse our consciences from acts that lead to death, so that we may serve the living God!
>
> For this reason Christ is the mediator of a new covenant, that those who are called may receive the promised eternal inheritance—now that he has died as a ransom to set them free from the sins committed under the first covenant. (Hebrews 9:7–15)

This issue goes to the very heart of Daniel's request: God's sanctuary on the holy hill and sacrifice for sin. Hebrews 9:24–28 describes the temple and sacrifice under the new covenant:

> For Christ did not enter a man-made sanctuary that was only a copy of the true one; he entered heaven itself, now to appear for us in God's presence. Nor did he enter heaven to offer himself again and again, the way the high priest enters the Most Holy Place every year with the blood that is not his own. Then Christ would have had to suffer many times since the creation of the world. But now he has appeared once for all at the end of the ages to do away with sin by the sacrifice of himself. Just as man is destined to die once, and after that to face judgment, so Christ was sacrificed once to take away the sins of many people.

In the seventy "sevens" prophecy, God was telling Daniel it would take 490 years for the new temple to be in place. That new temple is mentioned in the book of John, where Jesus Christ says,

> "Destroy this temple, and I will raise it again in three days."
> The Jews replied, "It has taken forty-six years to build this temple, and you are going to raise it in three days?" But the temple he had spoken of was his body. After he was raised from the dead, his disciples recalled what he had said. Then they believed the Scripture and the words that Jesus had spoken." (John 2:19–22)

The new temple was Jesus Christ, the place where God places His name, where one offering was made to cover sins, once for all. The apostle Paul says that all the animal sacrifices offered during the old covenant never really forgave sin, they merely pointed to the sacrifice that would—Jesus Christ. If the animal sacrifices had paid the penalty for sin, why would Christ have had to come at all? God wanted Israel to understand the concept of sacrifice and in so doing instituted a temporary covenant until a better one was in place.

Christ's sacrifice took care of the need to sacrifice animals at the temple, because, as we have said, He is now the temple, and He is also the sacrifice. In I Corinthians 5:7, it says, "Get rid of the old yeast that you may be a new batch without yeast—as you really are. For Christ, our Passover lamb, has been sacrificed." This is why John the Baptist, when he first sees Jesus says, "Look, the Lamb of God, who takes away the sin of the world!" John was proclaiming Christ as the eventual Passover lamb whose blood would save us from death. However, the place where God would dwell, or where He placed His name, would undergo a change on the Feast of Pentecost. On that day in AD 31, God filled His follow-ers with His Holy Spirit: God dwelling in man. This could only happen because those filled with the Spirit are "a new batch without yeast"—without sin due to the sacrifice of Jesus Christ. Those He has called are clean, and because of that, God now dwells in them—We have gone from a physical temple to a spiritual temple. So now those who have His Spirit are where God places His name, and they too are the temple, as it says in I Corinthians 3:16, 17: "Don't you know that you yourselves are God's temple and that God's Spirit lives in you? If anyone destroys God's temple, God will destroy him; for God's temple is sacred, and you are that temple." And again in verse 19, "Do you not know that your body is a temple of the Holy Spirit, who is in you, whom you have received from God?" And in Ephesians 2:19–22, Paul says,

> Consequently you are no longer foreigners and aliens, but fellow citizens with God's people and members of God's household, built on the foundation of the apostles and prophets, with Jesus Christ himself as the chief corner-stone. In him, the whole building is joined together and rises together to become a holy temple in the Lord. And in him you too are being built together to become a dwelling in which God lives by his Spirit."

Because these New Testament scriptures describe God's temple as the place where His Spirit dwells in His people, not a physical building, references to a temple post-Christ must be understood differently. The temple is not a building sitting on Mount Moriah where animal sacrifices are made, but the body of Christ, made up of people who are filled with the Spirit of God. Today, we call this the church.

To emphasize the point that the old temple with its system of animal sacrifices is unnecessary, God ended the seventy "sevens" prophecy saying, "And one who causes desolation will come upon the pinnacle of the abominable temple, until the end that is decreed is poured out on [it]." In verse 26, Gabriel says about the city and the sanctuary, "The end will come like a flood: War will continue until the end, and desolations have been decreed."

The "one who causes desolation" is none other than Satan because desolation occurs when people set up worship to other gods; Satan is the one who leads the world astray into deception. It's rather interesting that in Matthew 4:5–7, Satan and Jesus Christ are standing on the pinnacle of the temple. Ultimately, God is the one who changes where He places His name and discontinues the need for animal sacrifices through the sacrifice of His son. From that time on, God takes His name away from what was His temple and gives that piece of land over to abominable things—a dump, barren wasteland, and temples to other gods. Why does God do this? Because He has given us a new temple and a sacrifice that takes away sin once for all: Jesus Christ. It's no mistake that at the very hour of Christ's death, the curtain that separated the Holy of Holies from the temple "was torn in two" (Luke 23:45). It's at that very moment that the Most Holy Place became common, and within a mere thirty-eight or so years later, the whole temple completely ceased to exist. God removed the law and put in place only one way to atone for sin—the sacrifice of Jesus Christ. There is no other way. To this very day, those who keep the Law of Moses are in a state of suspension. On Passover and the Day of Atonement, they have no place to offer sacrifices because there is no temple on Mount Moriah; they remain in a covenant that cannot function as required, because God ended that covenant. Without the temple on Mount Moriah, the old covenant, as prescribed and regulated by scripture, is out of business.

There are some who believe the temple on Mount Moriah will be restored in the future. As we have just read, desolations will be in effect on Moriah until the end, and that's because there has been a change when it comes to the *true* temple and sacrifice—Jesus Christ. If, in the future, the temple and sacrifices are restored on Mount Moriah, it won't be by God—He no longer has a use for that system.

This new meaning to the idea of sanctuary and sacrifice helps us better understand what is being spoken of in Daniel 8:11, 12 where Daniel sees in a vision:

> It [the little horn] grew until it reached the host of the heavens, and it threw some of the starry host down to the earth and trampled on them. It set itself up to be as great as the Prince of the host; it took away the daily sacrifice from him, and the place of his sanctuary was brought low. Because of rebellion, the host of the saints and the daily sacrifice were given over to it. It prospered in everything it did, and truth was thrown to the ground.

Again, when Gabriel gives the interpretation (Daniel 8:19–26) of the vision of the evenings and mornings, he says, "He [meaning the stern-faced king] will cause astounding devastation and will succeed in whatever he does. He will destroy the mighty men and the holy people." The mighty men and the holy people are those who are filled with the Spirit of God—They are God's saints. Revelation 13:5–10 talks about the saints in the same end-time scenario:

> The beast was given a mouth to utter proud words and blasphemies and to exercise his authority for forty-two months. He opened his mouth to blaspheme God, and to slander his name and his dwelling place and those who

live in heaven. He was given power to make war against the saints and to conquer them. And he was given authority over every tribe, people, language and nation. All inhabitants of the earth will worship the beast—all whose names have not been written in the book of life belonging to the Lamb that was slain from the creation of the world.

It's the same discussion as one in Daniel 8 of a persecution of the saints. Daniel 11, starting in verse 31, says:

> "His [the king of the North's] armed forces will rise up to desecrate the temple fortress and will abolish the daily sacrifice. Then they will set up the abomination that causes desolation. With flattery he will corrupt those who have violated the covenant, but the people who know their God [the saints] will firmly resist him. Those who are wise will instruct many, though for a time they will fall by the sword or be burned or captured or plundered. When they fall, they will receive a little help, and many who are not sincere will join them. Some of the wise will stumble, so that they may be refined, purified and made spotless until the time of the end, for it will still come at the appointed time." (11:31–35).

The focus in these scriptures is the demise of the saints, or those who worship God. We are told in Revelation 8:3 that the prayers of the saints are offered with incense before the golden altar of God in heaven. In the new covenant, daily sacrifices are the prayers of the ones God has called, His church. Since all of the saints combined are the spiritual temple of God and their prayers are now the daily sacrifice, and the scriptures say they are going to be killed or imprisoned and handed over to the beast, it seems that this is the destruction of the temple and the taking away of the daily sacrifice spoken of in the new covenant. The focus of these scriptures is what happens to the saints, not what happens to a physical building. The saints at the end time are under tremendous persecution, so much so that the time period is called the "great tribulation." Christ said this time would be so bad that no other time period, before or after, is like it, and no one would survive if it were not cut short. But for the sake of the elect, or saints, it will be cut short.

What about 2 Thessalonians 2:3, 4 where it says, "Don't let anyone deceive you in any way, for that day will not come until the rebellion occurs and the man of lawlessness is revealed, the man doomed to destruction. He will oppose and will exalt himself over everything that is called God or is worshiped, so that he sets himself up in God's temple proclaiming himself to be God"? Or what about Matthew 24:15, 16 when Christ says, "So when you see standing in the holy place 'the abomination that causes desolation' spoken of through the prophet Daniel—let the reader understand—then those who are in Judea flee to the mountains." Don't these scriptures seem to indicate that the temple on Mount Moriah is rebuilt and that the end-time beast, or the man of lawlessness, has set himself up there to be worshiped? It is possible that the above-mentioned scriptures are talking about a final abomination that will be set up just before the return of Jesus Christ. It's also worth noting that these passages of scripture, mentioned above, were written while the temple was still intact on Moriah, and Moriah is still a place that God considers special because it's where His Son will return. The desolations, however, are still in effect until Christ returns. Nevertheless, this does not preclude the possibility of something like a temple replacing the Dome of the Rock now sitting on Mount Moriah. If that does occur, however, it is not something from God, but a continuation of the prophecy "desolations have been decreed." It does appear that the end-time beast will do something to replace the current Dome of the Rock, and many people will see this as a very good thing; they'll think they're worshiping God. However, this is a deception, and those who know their God will know that this is the fulfillment of the end-time prophecies mention above.

Mount Moriah will be the central point at the very end of this age because it is there that the end-time beast/stern-faced king will set up some type of worship. He will present himself as a priest-king, that is, both a religious leader and a national leader. In fact, there is every indication that this individual will set himself up as Jesus Christ, who is a priest-king, and will demand to be worshiped. Those who do not comply will be punished. All of this will take place because the desolation that has existed for at least two millennia will be close to ending. The good news is that Jesus Christ will come back, take His stand on the Mount of Olives (which is directly across from Mount Moriah), and with His resurrected saints destroy the final abomination. Then Jesus Christ will establish Himself and His throne on Mount Moriah and begin ruling the nations as the king of the kingdom of God. We are getting a little ahead of the story, but this gives some information as to the importance of Mount Moriah in the past and in the future. It's important to keep in mind the reason for the prophecy. Mount Moriah is the geographic center of the seventy "sevens" prophecy; it's what Daniel was concerned about in his prayer, so accordingly, the prophecy deals with that location alone. The other issue in Daniel's prayer is the forgiveness of sins, and that's dealt with on Mount Moriah as well, because that's where the sacrifice of Jesus Christ would eventually take place. And finally, Mount Moriah will be the place where Jesus Christ will "bring in everlasting righteousness" by establishing the kingdom of God—a fulfillment of the promise God made to Abraham back in Genesis 22:18: "… and through your offspring [Jesus Christ] all nations on earth will be blessed, because you have obeyed me." This prophecy serves as a compass, pointing us in the right direction for future events: Jesus Christ's ministry, His death, and the purpose of His death, several thousand years of desolation and war, and the hope of everlasting righteousness.

As we close one of the most intriguing prophecies of the Old Testament, it's important to keep in mind who the focus of this prophecy is: "the Anointed One, the ruler," Jesus Christ. All of this is revealed because Daniel is concerned with sin and the desolate city and holy hill. Sometimes in all the action that takes place in prophecy between nations and kings, it's hard to remember that the biggest concern God has is sin and the atonement for sin. Sin has been our biggest problem right from the beginning, and it's still the root cause of all of our problems today; it's what separates us from God. But God made a promise to Abraham and a great deal of His plan is revealed to Daniel in this prophecy. Although the prophecy essentially concludes with the death of Christ, the two main issues of the prophecy—Jesus Christ and the sanctuary—will play a large role in what is still yet to come, the greatest event of the age: the return of the Anointed One. The location of that great event, as we shall see in Chapter 12, is none other than Mount Moriah in the city that bears His name.

7

The Man Dressed in Linen

The seventy "sevens" prophecy gave Daniel a lot of information about what was to come, but it wasn't enough to soothe all of his concerns. He and his people were still in exile in Persia, and Daniel was still distressed about what was ahead. The seventy "sevens" described the future atonement of sin without a physical temple, but there was still a lot Daniel didn't know about the ultimate outcome of Israel. What would happen to his people?

Daniel is again given understanding about a message from God through a vision. This is the last vision in the book of Daniel, starting in Chapter 10 and ending in Chapter 12—the end of the book of Daniel. As we begin to read about this final vision, we see that it came to Daniel two years or so after the seventy "sevens" prophecy God gave through Gabriel.

> In the third year of Cyrus king of Persia, a revelation was given to Daniel (who was called Belteshazzar). Its message was true and it concerned a great war. The understanding of the message came to him in a vision. (Daniel 10:1)

Daniel commenced a period of mourning before and during the feast of Passover and Unleavened Bread.

> At that time I, Daniel, mourned for three weeks. I ate no choice food; no meat or wine touched my lips; and I used no lotions at all until the three weeks were over.
>
> On the twenty-fourth day of the first month, as I was standing on the bank of the great river Tigris, I looked up and there before me was a man dressed in linen, with the finest gold around his waist. His body was like chrysolite, his face like lightning, his eyes like flaming torches, his arms and legs like the gleam of burnished bronze, and his voice like the sound of a multitude. (Daniel 10:2, 3)

Assuming that Daniel was using the Hebrew calendar, the first month of the year is Abib, which usually corresponds to our late March or early to mid April. The first day of Abib is the first day of the calendar year; the tenth day commemorates the selection of the Passover lamb (Exodus 12:1–3); the fourteenth day is Passover, the time when the Passover lamb is slaughtered (Exodus 12:6); and the subsequent seven days make up the Feast of Unleavened Bread (Exodus 12:15–20). This time period is significant for the Jewish people and those who keep the law, even to this day. Passover and the Feast of Unleavened Bread commemorate the time when God led the captive Israelites out of slavery in Egypt. My speculation is that Daniel fasted during this time to call upon God to repeat that miraculous event and lead the Jewish people back to the Promised Land. It appears Daniel's fast ended on the last day of Unleavened Bread, the twenty-first day, and he probably figured that was the end of the matter so he went on about his business. However, three days later, he received a shocking answer to his concerns—probably greater than he could ever have imagined.

Who could this man be? Is this Gabriel again, or someone else from the angelic realm? To answer the question, I want to go to the books of Ezekiel and Revelation because the authors of these books are also prophets and they, too, saw a similar man.

> Then there came a voice from the expanse over their heads as they stood with lowered wings. Above the expanse over their heads was what looked like a throne of sapphire, and high above on the throne was a figure like that of a man. I saw that from what appeared to be his waist up he looked like glowing metal, as if full of fire, and that from there down he looked like fire; and brilliant light surrounded him. Like the appearance of a rainbow in the clouds on a rainy day, so was the radiance around him. This was the appearance of the likeness of the glory of the Lord. When I saw it, I fell face down, and I heard the voice of one speaking. He said to me, "Son of man, stand up on your feet and I will speak to you." (Ezekiel 1:25–2:1)

A similar description is given in two places in the book of Revelation:

> On the Lord's Day I was in the Spirit, and I heard behind me a loud voice like a trumpet, which said: "Write on a scroll what you see and send it to the seven churches: to Ephesus, Smyrna, Pergamum, Thyatira, Sardis, Philadelphia and Laodicea." I turned around to see the voice that was speaking to me. And when I turned I saw seven golden lampstands, and among the lampstands was someone "like a son of man" [Daniel 7:13] dressed in a robe reaching down to his feet and with a golden sash around his chest. His head and hair were white

like wool, as white as snow, and his eyes were like blazing fire. His feet were like bronze glowing in a furnace, and his voice was like the sound of rushing waters. In his right hand he held seven stars, and out of his mouth came a sharp double-edged sword. His face was like the sun shining in all its brilliance. When I saw him, I fell at his feet as though dead. Then he placed his right hand on me and said: "Do not be afraid. I am the First and the Last. I am the Living One; I was dead, and behold I am alive for ever and ever! And I hold the keys of death and Hades." (Revelation 1:10–18)

I saw heaven standing open and there before me was a white horse, whose rider is called Faithful and True. With justice he judges and makes war. His eyes are like blazing fire, and on his head are many crowns. He has a name written on him that no one knows but he himself. He is dressed in a robe dipped in blood, and his name is the Word of God. The armies of heaven were following him, riding on white horses and dressed in fine linen, white and clean. Out of his mouth comes a sharp sword with which to strike down the nations. "He will rule them with an iron scepter." He treads the winepress of the fury of the wrath of God Almighty. On his robe and on his thigh he has this name written: King of Kings and Lord of Lords. (Revelation 19:11–16)

It appears from the scriptures above that "the man dressed in linen" is none other than the Word of God who ultimately came down to earth and dwelt among us in the flesh. I don't believe this is Gabriel because in Chapter 9 when Daniel sees Gabriel, he recognizes him from an earlier vision (Chapter 8). There is also much more fear and awe when Daniel sees this man in Chapter 10. I believe what he sees here is the very presence of God.

I, Daniel, was the only one who saw the vision; the men with me did not see it, but such terror overwhelmed them that they fled and hid themselves. So I was left alone, gazing at this great vision; I had no strength left, my face turned deathly pale and I was helpless. Then I heard him speaking, and as I listened to him, I fell into a deep sleep, my face to the ground. A hand touched me and set me trembling on my hands and knees. He said, "Daniel, you who are highly esteemed, consider carefully the words I am about to speak to you, and stand up, for I have now been sent to you." And when he said this to me, I stood up trembling. (Daniel 10:7–11)

You might ask, if this was the presence of God, who would have sent Him to speak to Daniel? In John 1:1–4, we see how God has existed: "In the beginning was the Word, and the Word was with God, and the Word was God. He was with God in the beginning. Through him all things were made; without him nothing was made that has been made. In him was life, and that life was the light of men." At the same time, the Bible teaches there is only *one* God: "'The most important [commandment],' answered Jesus, 'is this: "Hear, O Israel, the Lord our God, the Lord is one. Love the Lord your God with all your heart and with all your soul and with all your mind and with all your strength"'" (Mark 12:29, 30). The Word was also active throughout the Old Testament period. Paul says in I Corinthians 10:1–5: "For I do not want you to be ignorant of the fact, brothers, that our forefathers were all under the cloud and they all passed through the sea. They were all baptized into Moses in the cloud and the sea. They all ate the same spiritual food and drank the same spiritual drink; for they drank from the spiritual rock that accompanied them, and that rock was Christ." The Word of God, who later came down in the flesh and was known as Jesus Christ, accompanied Israel out of Egypt and through the desert. John 1:14 describes the coming of the Anointed One as prophesied in the seventy "sevens": "The Word became flesh and made his dwelling among us. We have seen his glory, the glory of the One and Only who came from the Father, full of grace and truth." And verse 18 tells us who the presence of God is in the Old Testament: "No one has ever seen God, but the One and Only begotten Son, who is at the Father's side, has made him known." Jesus Christ reemphasizes this point in John 6:46: "It is written in the Prophets: 'They will all be taught by God.' Everyone who listens to the Father and learns from him comes to me. No one has seen the Father except the one who is from God; only he has seen the Father."

Only Jesus Christ, the Word, has seen the Father, and His work is to reveal the Father and actively take part in His plans for His creation: to bless all nations through Abraham's seed. But it's important to remember that God and Jesus Christ are One, not two. And now, in Chapter 10, the man dressed in linen—the Word of God—is about to reveal much of that plan to Daniel.

The Word, in a vision, says to Daniel:

> Do not be afraid, Daniel. Since the first day that you set your mind to gain understanding and to humble yourself before your God, your words were heard, and I have come in response to them. But the prince of the Persian kingdom resisted me twenty-one days. Then Michael, one of the chief princes, came to help me, because I was detained there with the king of Persia. (Daniel 10:12, 13)

Who is the man dressed in linen talking about? Who are these people: "the prince of the Persian kingdom," "Michael, one of the chief princes," and "the king of Persia"? Let's start with what we know. Michael is identified by name and as a chief prince. In the same chapter in verse 21, it says, "... (No one supports me against them except Michael, your prince ...)" Michael is again mentioned in Daniel 12:1: "At that time Michael, the great prince who protects your people, will arise ..." Michael is mentioned two more times by name. Jude 9 says, "But even the archangel Michael, when he was disputing with the devil about the body of Moses, did not dare to bring a slanderous accusation against him, but said, 'The Lord rebuke you!'" The last reference is in Revelation 12:7, 8: "And there was war in heaven. Michael and his angels fought against the dragon, and the dragon and his angels fought back. But he was not strong enough, and they lost their place in heaven." So we know that Michael is a chief prince who protects Daniel's people, an archangel (or chief angel), and he has angels under him. His duties are that of a warrior on God's side, against Satan. So we now know who one prince is.

A second prince is spoken of: "the prince of the Persian kingdom." If Michael, an archangel, is given the title "prince," then it would make sense the other prince is also a powerful spirit being. This prince resists the Word, and right there we should know who he's from. Who throughout the Bible resists God? In John 14:28–31, Christ, before He is about to be handed over, suffer, and die, says, "You heard me say, 'I am going away, and I am coming back to you.' If you loved me, you would be glad that I am going to the Father, for the Father is greater than I. I told you now before it happens, so when it does happen you will believe. I will not speak with you much longer, for the prince of this world is coming. He has no hold over me, but the world must learn that I love the Father and I do exactly as my Father has commanded me." The "prince of this world" is part of the same force we see detaining the Word from coming to Daniel. The references to Michael in Jude and Revelation show Satan the devil resisting one of God's chief angels. Again, in I Thessalonians 2:18, Satan resists God's people as they do His work: "For we wanted to come to you—certainly I, Paul, did, again and again—but Satan stopped us." Revelation 12:4 says, speaking of Satan, "His tail swept a third of the stars out of the sky and flung them to the earth ..." and verse 9 says, "The great dragon was hurled down—that ancient serpent called the devil, or Satan, who leads the whole world astray. He was hurled to the earth, and his angels with him." So Satan and his demons are the ones who resist God and His angels. Throughout the Bible, we see that Satan constantly tries to disrupt God's plans.

And we have already been introduced to the other angel named in the book of Daniel: Gabriel. In Daniel 8:15, 16, it says, "While I, Daniel, was watching the vision and trying to understand it, there before me stood one who looked like a man. And I heard a man's voice from the Ulai calling, 'Gabriel, tell this man the meaning of the vision.'" The other reference in Daniel is 9:20–22: "While I was speaking and praying, confessing my sin and the sin of my people Israel and making my request to the Lord my God for his holy hill—while I was still in prayer, Gabriel, the man I had seen in the earlier vision, came to me in swift flight about the time of the evening sacrifice. He instructed me and said to me, 'Daniel, I have now come to give you insight and understanding.'"

Gabriel is also referred to in Luke 1:11, 13, speaking to Zechariah, the father of John the Baptist: "Then an angel of the Lord appeared to him, standing at the right side of the altar of incense … But the angel said to him: 'Do not be afraid, Zechariah; your prayer has been heard. Your wife Elizabeth will bear you a son, and you are to give him the name John.'" A few verses later, we find out who this angel is: "The angel answered, 'I am Gabriel. I stand in the presence of God, and I have been sent to speak to you and to tell you this good news …'" (verse 19). The last time Gabriel is mentioned by name is one of the most famous passages of the Bible: "In the sixth month, God sent the angel Gabriel to Nazareth, a town in Galilee, to a virgin pledged to be married to a man named Joseph, a descendant of David. The virgin's name was Mary. The angel went to her and said, 'Greetings, you who are highly favored! The Lord is with you'" (verses 26–28). It appears that Michael is the chief protector and soldier of God's people, and Gabriel is the chief messenger, or herald, of God. The fact that both of these chief princes appear to Daniel signifies the importance of what is going on in the events of Daniel's life.

Now, back to Daniel 10:13. You might ask, "How could Satan detain the Word of God?" It's hard to know for sure, but it may be that Satan brought accusations against God's people similar to the type of discussion recorded in the biblical book of Job. In Chapter 1:6–12, it says,

> One day the angels came to present themselves before the Lord, and Satan also came with them. The Lord said to Satan, "Where have you come from?"
>
> Satan answered the Lord, "From roaming through the earth and going back and forth in it."
>
> Then the Lord said to Satan, "Have you considered my servant Job? There is no one on earth like him; he is blameless and upright, a man who fears God and shuns evil."
>
> "Does Job fear God for nothing?" Satan replied. "Have you not put a hedge around him and his household and everything he has? You have blessed the work of his hands, so that his flocks and herds are spread throughout the land. But stretch out your hand and strike everything he has, and he will surely curse you to your face."

> The Lord said to Satan, "Very well, then, everything he has is in your hands, but on the man himself do not lay a finger." Then Satan went out from the presence of the Lord.

Here, Satan is given power over God's servant, to do what he wants. In Daniel 10, perhaps Satan was going to do harm against something God wanted protected and that detained the Word with the king of Persia until the matter was resolved. We don't know exactly what happened except that Michael came and helped the Word so He could come and explain future events to Daniel. Satan knew the importance of the message Daniel was to hear and did everything he could to prevent the message from being delivered. All of this underscores the enormous activity that takes place in the spirit world, and we only get a small glimpse of it here in these scriptures.

As we continue in verse 14 of Chapter 10 we learn the reason Daniel receives a visit from God: "Now I have come to explain to you what will happen to your people in the future, for the vision concerns a time yet to come." The "people" the Word is referring to is most likely the Jews, or the whole house of Israel. It was probably their future Daniel was fasting about earlier in the chapter. But as the prophecy continues, this term takes on new meaning. The term "future" seems to indicate the end times, or the latter days, but it may just explain the time the vision leads to, or concludes in. This vision concludes, or is fulfilled, with the most important event in the mind of every Israelite since around 586 BC—the restoration of the house of Israel in the land promised to Abraham.

Even though Daniel had experienced awesome events—interpreting dreams, dealing with the rise and fall of kings and kingdoms, having chief angels bring him incredible visions, being thrown into a chamber of death filled with lions—the occurrence of this vision seemed to terrify him the most.

> While he [the Word] was saying this to me, I bowed with my face toward the ground and was speechless. Then one who looked like a man [or "Then something that looked like a man's hand"] touched my lips, and I opened my mouth and began to speak. I said to the one standing before me, "I am overcome with anguish because of the vision, my lord, and I am helpless. How can I, your servant, talk with you, my lord? My strength is gone and I can hardly breathe. (Daniel 10:15–17)

The prophet Isaiah had a very similar experience when he talked with God as recorded in Isaiah 6:4–7: "At the sound of their [the angels'] voices the doorposts and thresholds shook and the temple was filled with smoke. 'Woe to me!' I cried.

'I am ruined! For I am a man of unclean lips, and I live among a people of unclean lips, and my eyes have seen the King, the Lord Almighty.' Then one of the seraphs flew to me with a live coal in his hand, which he had taken with tongs from the altar. With it he touched my mouth and said, 'See, this has touched your lips; your guilt is taken away and your sin atoned for.'"

The apostle John describes a similar situation while on the island of Patmos. "When I saw him, I fell at his feet as though dead. Then he placed his right hand on me and said: 'Do not be afraid. I am the First and the Last. I am the Living One; I was dead, and behold I am alive for ever and ever!" (Revelation 1:17, 18). From these passages, it appears that when mere human beings are in the presence of God in His glory, they are overwhelmed almost to the point of death, but God helps them stand in His presence.

> Again the one who looked like a man touched me and gave me strength. "Do not be afraid, O man highly esteemed," he said. "Peace! Be strong now; be strong."
> When he spoke to me, I was strengthened and said, "Speak my lord, since you have given me strength." (Daniel 10:18, 19)

Before He outlines the future, He again points out the forces behind the scene in the spirit world that war against what is seen: "Soon I will return to fight against the prince of Persia, and when I go the prince of Greece will come; but first I will tell you what is written in the Book of Truth. (No one supports me against them except Michael, your prince. And in the first year of Darius the Mede, I took my stand to support and protect him)" (Daniel 10:20–11:1). It reminds me of what the apostle Paul said in Ephesians 6:12: "For our struggle is not against flesh and blood, but against the rulers, against the authorities, against the powers of this dark world and against the spiritual forces of evil in the heavenly realms." It is important for us to keep in mind that there are spiritual forces that play a large role in the events we see happening before our eyes.

After Persia fell, Greece became a world-ruling country. The Word talks about Michael helping Him fight against these demonic forces. Apparently, from what is said here, God intervenes to support Darius's reign in his first year. Why? Well, my speculation is God intervenes so that His plan and prophecy are accomplished. I think He tells Daniel this because He is about to explain a 2,500-year prophecy; He wants Daniel to know He'll intervene, accomplishing everything He's said He'll accomplish. Also, during this time, Darius was ruling over the remnant of God's nation Israel, so I'm sure Satan and his crowd wanted to do as much harm as they could to God's plan and the remnant of His people. Satan still leads the nations astray (Revelation 12:9 confirms that, saying: "The great dragon was hurled down—that ancient serpent called the devil, or Satan, who leads the whole world astray."), but God intervenes, apparently in some kind of a struggle, to make sure His plan is accomplished. Michael, who plays an incredible role later on in the prophecy in Chapters 11 and 12, is the one who helps the Word battle against these wicked forces. This is one of the few times we get to see a glimpse into the battles that go on behind the scenes, and I am sure it is just as active, if not more so, today!

So in Daniel 10:20, the Word asks Daniel, "Do you know why I have come to you?" The answer to the question has already been given in verse 14: "Now I have come to explain to you what will happen to your people in the future, for the vision concerns a time yet to come." As we begin looking at this long prophecy describing events between the kings of the North and South, it's worth noting that it takes awhile—fourteen verses—for any mention of Daniel's people and then another eighteen verses before we see them mentioned again, so we go through a lot of world history before we find out what will happen to Daniel's people. We are introduced to two kings who are the focus of the prophecy, one from the North and one from the South. These kings are the remnants of the Greek empire after the fall of Alexander. The Bible capitalizes the titles North and South because they represent formal empires. These two kings are really what will become two great empires; they are still very much in existence today. From time to time, I will go back to the statue of Chapter 2 and the beasts of Chapter 7 to compare with this chronology in Chapter 11. Remember, there are only four empires in Chapters 2 and 7, and they should line up with what is forecast here in Chapter 11. The prophecy of the kings from the North and South starts around 536 BC (when Daniel is being told of these events) and ends at the second coming of Jesus Christ and the resurrection of His saints, so these kings, or empires, have to exist over this long stretch of time. Also, the main focus is on the king of the North. He will be the one at the end who rises up and kills the saints, as we saw in Chapters 7 and 8. The key to understanding this prophecy is to know the real focus is on what happens at the end of the age. Back in Chapter 7, Daniel wants to know more about the fourth beast, its ten horns, and the little horn that speaks boastfully, and almost the entire prophecy in Chapter 11 is an answer to that request. Of the forty-five verses of Chapter 11, thirty-one are dedicated to the events in the end-time period. That means only fourteen verses are dedicated to over 2,500 years. In order to do that, the prophecy skips through large spans of time.

So with all of this in mind, let's start the 2,500-year prophesy of "the kings of the North and South." The Word of God, who is talking to Daniel, says in verse two of Chapter 11, "Now then, I tell you the truth: Three more kings will appear in Persia, and then a fourth, who will be far richer than all the others. When he has gained power by his wealth, he will stir up everyone against the kingdom of Greece." Assuming this prophesy was given around 536 BC, three more kings did appear after Cyrus, who died in 529 BC: Cambyses, who ruled from 529–522 BC; Gaumata, disguised as Smerdis, the king's dead brother, who ruled in 522 BC; and Darius the Great, who ruled from 521–486 BC. Then a fourth, mighty king, Xerxes (who ruled from 486–465 BC) appeared and attacked the burgeoning kingdom of Greece.

> Xerxes (the AHASUERUS of Ezra and Esther), who had gained experience as viceroy of Babylon, lacked the tolerance of his predecessor and treated harshly both Egypt and Babylon. He would have preferred to direct his energies toward building palaces and monuments, but the Greek problem would not go away. In 480 BC, a Persian army accompanied by ships manned by Phoenician, Ionian, Egyptian, and Cypriot allies moved against Greece. A canal was dug through the isthmus of Sane to avoid the dangerous promontory of Athos. After a delay at Thermopylae, Thebes and Athens were taken by the Persians, but the Greeks inflicted a disastrous defeat on the Persian fleet at Salamis, then near Miletus, and again at Plataea and Mycale. Xerxes was forced to relinquish everything beyond Asia Minor. He was assassinated in his palace in 465 BC.[6]

So verse two of Chapter 11 happened just as God said it would. After Xerxes, the Persian empire began a rapid decline.

Now on to verses 3 and 4:

> Then a mighty king will appear, who will rule with great power and do as he pleases. After he has appeared, his empire will be broken up and parceled out toward the four winds of heaven. It will not go to his descendants, nor will it have the power he exercised, because his empire will be uprooted and given to others.

In 336 BC, Alexander the Great ascended to the throne of Greece and from 334 to 327 BC, he conquered everything from Greece all the way down to Egypt and all the way to India. He is known as one of the "greatest military geniuses of all times."[7] Interestingly, after all of his conquests, Alexander intended to make the city of Babylon, of all places, the supreme capital of his entire empire. "While engaged in this work (preparing Babylon) he was seized with malaria, which aggravated by his recklessness in eating and drinking, took his life in his thirty-third year (323 BC)."[8] After Alexander's death, there were a series of wars called the Diadochi wars. These wars, in which many of Alexander's kin and generals were involved, dealt with filling the vacuum of power left after Alexander's death. The term "the four winds of heaven" used in verse four does not necessarily mean the kingdom was divided into four parts. The Diadochi wars last at least twenty-three years, and they really weren't settled for another twenty years after that, so it's a bit limiting to jump to the conclusion that the empire was divided into four sections, as some believe. Besides, the prophecy eventually brings us to two kings, North and South, and they're the kingdoms we want to identify.

It is here that our book takes a different chronology than what most churches believe. Conventional thought has this prophecy concluding in Chapter 11 with Antiochus Epiphanies, who died in 166 BC. Antiochus Epiphanies was a Seleucid from Syria who conquered Jerusalem and brought about a terrible persecution of the Jews. Although some of his actions mirror what is later talked about in Chapter 11, there are reasons that we will detail later that disqualify him from being the person described in the Bible. Many believe Chapter 11 jumps from the 160s BC to the return of Christ and the resurrection of the saints. I don't believe God spends all that time in Chapter 11 dealing with wars between the Ptolemaic and Seleucid kingdoms and then dead-ends in the middle of nowhere in 166 BC. That would leave us with nothing. It's important to remember that Chapters 11 and 12 start with Daniel in Persia in the third year of Cyrus, around 336 BC, and end with the resurrection of the saints and the return of Jesus Christ. With that in mind, I believe all the events mentioned between Chapters 11:5 and 12:3 are events that occur between those dates—337 BC and the end of the age. The flow of events brings us to the end-time resurrection, and it also lines up with the beasts of Chapter 7 and the statue in Chapter 2. This last prophecy is a reflection and magnification of the fourth beast and the iron legs and toes of iron mixed with clay of the statue. Furthermore, this prophecy also has to reflect the events of Chapter 8, which also involves two empires: one from "Greece," or the goat with the prominent horn, and the kings of "Media and Persia," or the ram with two horns. Since the ram and the goat represent two empires in the "time of wrath," or the end time, it gives us a future view of what is meant by the kings of the North and South. By future, I mean from the viewpoint of someone living in 323 BC.

Before we go on to verses five and six, we should review the empires of the statue in Chapter 2, and the beasts of Chapter 7. Babylon is the first empire, followed by Media/Persia, and then Greece. After these, there's only one empire left—Rome—and because Chapter 11's focus is on the king of the North, we can conclude that the king of the North is Rome and her successor states. By plugging in Rome and her successors as the king of the North, we can take Chapter 11 to the present and beyond. If this isn't true, we can only go as far as 166 BC where many believe Chapter 11 essentially ends, making this chapter of no importance for today. However, the bulk of Chapter 11 deals with the end-time beast and the saints, so at least half of the chapter is still yet to occur. This makes Chapter 11 very useful and relevant to the saints now and in the future—which is the reason God is giving Daniel the prophecy in the first place. ("Now I have come to explain to you what will happen to your people in the future.") It's very important to remember that Chapters 2, 7, 8, 11, and 12 all tie in together—and they all end with the return of Jesus Christ. Chapter 8 and 11 are an answer to Daniel's request to know more about the fourth beast of Chapter 7, and it is with this thought that we begin to look at verses five and six in Chapter 11.

> The king of the South will become strong, but one of his commanders will become even stronger than he and will rule his own kingdom with great power. After some years, they will become allies. The daughter of the king of the South will go to the king of the North to make an alliance, but she will not retain her power, and he and his power [or offspring] will not last. In those days she will be handed over, together with her royal escort and her father [or her child] and the one who supported her. (Daniel 11:5, 6 see footnote *b* in NIV)

After Alexander the Great of Greece died, his empire was broken up into several parts and led by the Ptolemys of Egypt, the Seleucids of Damascus, the Antigonids of Macedonia, Lysimachus of Asia Minor, and Cassander of Macedonia and Greece. However, Chapter 11 only deals with the dichotomy of North and South, and this dichotomy, if we understand it correctly, lasts at least 2,300 years or so from the fall of Greece on into the future. I would like to focus on the sentence, "After some years they will become allies," because it's here I think we can begin to understand who the North and South are. I believe this event is talking about the time when Cleopatra went to Julius Caesar and then Mark Antony to make an alliance. When the scripture mentions "one of his commanders," it's talking about one of Alexander's commanders, not the king of the South's. The northernmost part of Alexander's empire, the Antigonids, was ultimately folded into the new European superpower, Rome, around 168 BC. When in verse five it mentions, "one of his commanders will become stronger than he and will rule his own kingdom with great power," the "he" is Alexander and the only kingdom stronger than his was Rome. I believe this is the transition from the third to the fourth beast, or the thighs of bronze to the legs of iron. By the time of Cleopatra, Julius Caesar, and Mark Antony, Alexander's empire was, for the most part, being broken up into two parts: the European Romans and the Egyptian/Arab world. The Ptolemys and the Seleucids were eventually folded into a sort of pan-Arab arrangement. But before we go any further, let's take a look at verse six of Chapter 11.

Cleopatra was forced from the throne of Egypt by her brother Ptolemy XII and driven into exile in Syria. It is there Cleopatra joined an alliance with Julius Caesar and in 47 BC defeated and killed Ptolemy XII. Caesar proclaimed Cleopatra queen of Egypt. They had a son, Ptolemy XIII, but after Caesar's assassination, Cleopatra is alleged to have poisoned and killed their son. After Caesar's assassination, Cleopatra became involved with Mark Antony, a Roman general and one-third emperor, and she bore him twins. Eventually, Antony became involved in the losing end of a civil war and he, Cleopatra, and their son, died in 30 BC.[9] Egypt, "her royal estate," was "handed over" and became a Roman province, and the "one who supported her" was also "handed over." As we proceed in Chapter 11, we begin to see the dichotomy of North and South manifested in a European Christian "North" and an Arabian Islamic "South." This distinction will carry us through the entire prophecy right up to the present.

> One from her family line will arise to take her place. He will attack the forces of the king of the North and enter his fortress; he will fight against them and be victorious. He will also seize their gods, their metal images and their valuable articles of silver and gold and carry them off to Egypt. (Daniel 11:7, 8)

I must say verses 7 and 8 present some difficulty. First of all, the Ptolemaic dynasty essentially came to an end with Cleopatra's death, and there doesn't seem to be any genetic connection to any future rulers of Egypt, unless it is through her mother's line. "Family line" could also mean one who inherits the throne of Egypt, or one who inherits the kingdom of the South. The King James Bible says, "But out of a branch of her roots one shall stand up in his estate." It's possible that there is no way to know the connection between Cleopatra and the "one" to whom they are referring, just like without the Bible, it would be difficult to connect Jesus Christ to Abraham. I must admit this is a weak point in this forensic on Chapter 11.

With all of this in mind, I would like to take a look at some historical events that take place from 638–1009 to see if they can shed light on understanding this prophecy. I would first like to talk about the word "fortress" used in verse 7. If Rome is the king of the North, "fortress" cannot mean Rome itself because no force from the South ever entered the Eternal City, so it has to mean something else altogether. Since Jerusalem is what was on Daniel's mind, and it is what becomes the most prized possession in the Middle East over the next 1,500 years, I believe the word "fortress" is synonymous with Jerusalem, or perhaps the Temple Mount itself. In 614, Chosroes II conquered Jerusalem from Byzantine/Roman rule and carried off what was supposed to be the true cross and destroyed the most sacred Christian shrine, the Church of the Holy Sepulcher. Chosroes II was also known as a pharaoh of Egypt because he conquered the country. Chosroes II was a Persian, and his empire, at its height, essentially comprised the area the Ptolemys and the Seleucids once ruled. In 630, the Roman emperor Heraclius recaptured Jerusalem for the Byzantines/Romans and restored the Church of the Holy Sepulcher. What we are beginning to see is the dichotomy of Middle Eastern empires and European empires, or in other terms, the dichotomy of the Moslems and Christians. The Middle Eastern countries were ruled by Persians, then Moslem Arabs; the Europeans were ruled by Rome and then her Christian successor states.

In 638, Caliph Omar conquered Jerusalem and extended Arab/Moslem rule all the way to Egypt. Omar cleared the Temple Mount, where the temple to Jupiter once stood, and built a small mosque. In 687, Caliph Abd al-Malik began construction on the Dome of the Rock, and construction was completed in 691. To this day, the shrine sits atop Mount Moriah on the very place Solomon's temple, and two subsequent temples, served as a worship site for the Living God. From 691 to 1009, Jerusalem, for the most part, was a Moslem and Christian holy place under the control of the Moslem Arabs. In 1009, Caliph Hakim of Egypt, leader of a radical Shiite sect, took over Jerusalem and destroyed the Church of the Holy Sepulcher and most likely carried away any valuable objects back to Egypt. For about sixty years, Christian and Jewish worship was banned. This act is what many believe was the genesis for what eventually led to the king of the North's retaliation.

For the most part, I have used the New International Version (NIV) translation when referring to the Bible; however, in the case of Daniel 11:9, I think the King James (KJ) translation may express the point more accurately. The NIV says in verse 9, "Then the king of the North will invade the realm of the king of the South but will retreat to his own country." I don't think it makes a whole lot of sense that the king of the North would invade but then retreat. The KJ says, "So the king of the south shall come into his [the king of the north's?] kingdom and shall return into his own land." In other words, the king of the South will invade Jerusalem and return Jerusalem to his own land, or he will simply return to his own homeland having conquered Jerusalem for his empire. From 630 to 1099, the king of the South invaded and maintained control of the Holy Land. But after Hakim and the Seljuk Turks prohibited Christian worship, there was anger in the kingdom of the North, which leads us to verse 10. If you use the NIV translation in verse 9, there is no historical event that is parallel. The Europeans never went to Jerusalem to invade and then retreat. Also, Daniel 11 is really not interested in internecine squabbles within each empire's structure. In other words, when the Seljuk Turks overthrew Caliph Hakim, there is no record of the event in Daniel, because Jerusalem and the surrounding area were still under Islamic control. The whole focus of Daniel 11 is noting when control of Jerusalem is shifted from the North to the South, or vice versa.

Now to verse 10:

> His sons [the king of the North's] will prepare for war and assemble a great army, which will sweep on like an irresistible flood and carry the battle as far as his fortress.

In 1096, Pope Urban II commenced the Crusades that were comprised of English, French, Italian, and eventually some German soldiers. In 1099, the king of the North's armies took control of Jerusalem from the king of the South and held power there until 1187. In 1187, the forces of the king of the South fought back and recaptured Jerusalem. There was a second and third Crusade that retook Jerusalem from the king of the South. All in all, the crusader period lasted about two hundred fifty years, which is the essence of verse 10.

Now for a quick recap before we go any further. Jerusalem fell into the domain of Alexander the Great around 330 BC. When he died, his kingdom was divided up and Jerusalem fell into the southern (South) sphere of his empire. Around 62 BC, Pompey (North) came down and occupied Jerusalem, and around 49 BC, Julius Caesar made a pact with Cleopatra so that for a short time, the North and the South were allied together. After Cleopatra's death, Jerusalem stayed within the Roman Empire (Jesus Christ had his ministry and was crucified during this time period). In 330, Emperor Constantine declared the Roman Empire for Christianity, and the Byzantine Christians (North) maintained control of Jerusalem until 614. In 614, Chosroes conquered Jerusalem, and except for a brief few years between 628–638, the city was in the hands of the king of the South, who had become a follower of the prophet Mohammed. At this point, the North was a Christian empire headed by a Roman Pope and the South was an Islamic empire divided, after Mohammed's death, into Shiite and Sunni sects. From 638 to 1099, the king of the South controlled Jerusalem. In 1099, Jerusalem was recaptured for the North for about ninety years. In 1187, Jerusalem was conquered by Saladin who returned Jerusalem to the king of the South; however, over the next one hundred fifty years, there would be further skirmishes and Jerusalem would be retaken by the North in a second (1229–1239) and third (1243–1244) attempt. All of this history is covered in Daniel 11:4–10.

> Then the king of the South will march out in a rage and fight against the king of the North, who will raise a large army, but it will be defeated. When the army is carried off, the king of the South will be filled with pride and will slaughter many thousands, yet he will not remain triumphant. (Daniel 11:11, 12)

Here, the Islamic empire entered into an area held by the Christian empire. "In 1244 Jerusalem was sacked by Kwarizmian Tartars, and in 1247 the city fell to Egypt under the Ayyubids. But in 1249 Aybak, a mamluk (a former slave), began a rule that was to last for nearly three centuries. The Mamelukes were peoples brought from Russia, the Caucasus, and central Asia by the Caliphs of Baghdad to serve as soldier slaves. They had gained great power, and Jerusalem came under that power." Then in 1517, Selim took Jerusalem for the Ottoman Empire. The Ottoman Empire was perhaps the greatest Islamic-based empire the world has ever known. At its height, the empire stretched from Central Europe throughout all of the Mediterranean Sea, Libya, Egypt, Syria, Jordan, Iraq, and Turkey. It began to dissolve around the mid-nineteenth century and was, believe it or not, one of the primary causes of World War I; its decline and pending vacuum of power was known as the "Eastern Question."

All of the expanding European colonial powers (the Christian Empire) were pondering the question: Who is going to be the recipient of the lands of the Ottoman Empire when it collapses? For a while, it appeared Germany was going to be the big winner, but we're getting ahead of the story, so I'll go back to the glory of the Ottomans. No non-Christian empire ever posed such a threat to the Christian empire as did the Ottomans in the fifteenth and sixteenth centuries; their empire went as far as modern-day Bosnia. Suffice it to say, this was the king of the South's greatest hour, but as the end of verse 12 says, "yet he will not remain triumphant," and as we shall see, he did not.

As a reminder, the Bible is skipping through 300–500 year spans of history because the real focus of Daniel 11 is the events that happen at the very end of the age. Half of Chapter 11 is dedicated to the end time, and as we begin to approach that point, we can bring in the events chronicled in Chapter 8 and some of 7, as a parallel account.

As a prelude to verse 13, I would like to describe the events leading up to the end of World War I, the dissolution of the Ottoman Empire, and—for the first time in five hundred years—the arrival of the king of the North in Jerusalem. At the beginning of the twentieth century, Germany was looking to expand her empire as Britain, France, and others had done through colonization. The problem was that most of the world had been colonized leaving very little left for Germany. However, the decaying Ottoman Empire was a place where Germany found some opportunity and began a relationship by building the Berlin-to-Baghdad railway. The Ottoman Empire was headquartered in Constantinople, Turkey, just like the British Empire was headquartered in London. When World War I broke out, Turkey allied itself with Germany. At the close of the war, the British, under Colonel Allenby, entered Jerusalem. Germany was forced to sign an armistice, and Turkey, being on the losing side, had to surrender most of her empire, and part of that empire was the land of Palestine and the city of Jerusalem.

We now arrive at verse 13 of Daniel 11:

> For the king of the North will muster another army, larger than the first; and after several years, he will advance with a huge army fully equipped.

This brings us to Jerusalem under the Balfour Declaration of 1917. The declaration, endorsed by the newly formed League of Nations, stated that this land called Palestine would be the place for a Jewish homeland, and the British would be the administrators of the mandate. For the next thirty years, the British tried to administer Palestine under the new British mandate; however, the Arabs and the Jews, and newly arriving Jewish immigrants from Europe, were in conflict about who would occupy and control the land.

Verse 14 describes this very time:

> In those times many will rise against the king of the South. The violent men among your own people will rebel in fulfillment of the vision, but without success.

This was a time of great strife between Arabs and Jews. Several times, there was fierce conflict between the two groups. The latter part of this verse is very interesting. What does it mean when it says, "The violent men among your own people will rebel in fulfillment of the vision"? What vision? Well, way back in Chapter 10 verse 14, it says, "Now I have come to explain to you what will happen to your people in the future, for the vision concerns a time yet to come." The fulfillment of the vision is what happens at the end of the vision, or the completion of the vision. In order to see that, we have to skip ahead to Chapter 12 where Michael, the great prince who protects the Jewish people, will arise and everyone whose name is written in the book of life will be delivered. We know from Jesus Christ and prophecies in the Bible that the land of Israel promised to Abraham will be established at that time. The last conversation between the apostles and Jesus Christ in Acts 1:6, 7 deals with this very point:

> So when they [the Apostles and Christ] met together they asked him, "Lord, are you at this time going to restore the kingdom to Israel?"
> He said to them: "It is not for you to know the times and dates the Father has set by his own authority. But you will receive power when the Holy Spirit comes on you; and you will be my witnesses in Jerusalem, and in all Judea and Samaria, and to all the ends of the earth."

So, what the latter part of Daniel 11:14 is describing is the Jewish people trying to do this through violent means, but, as the Bible says, they will not have success. God has established the time for the fulfillment of the vision, and man cannot speed it up or bring it about on his own. From 1917 to 1947, the British tried to peacefully control Palestine, but there was no formal Jewish state. After the Holocaust occurred during World War II, many felt the need for a Jewish homeland. So in 1948, the United Nations, which at that time was totally dominated by the Christian nations of France, Britain, and the United States, declared that part of Palestine become the Jewish state of Israel. However, the city of Jerusalem was not part of the new Jewish state and was declared an international or neutral city that essentially remained in the hands of the king of the South.

The new nation of Israel would need a lot of help to get started and survive the turbulent and hostile Middle East. The new state was not a welcomed sight for her Arab neighbors. But, with an enormous amount of aid from the U.S. and Britain, the new country thrived. The most important asset the Christian kingdom (U.S., Britain, and France) could provide was military supplies and weapons. Israel had access to the most advanced weaponry in the world, so when she was attacked, Israel could defend herself. Because Israel received so much monetary and military help from the Christian kingdom, the rest of the world considered it part of that kingdom. Israel was really a Western nation in the Middle East. It had a Western-style democratic government and a western-style economy; it was Western in culture, and, most importantly, it had a Western-style military. The only un-Western thing about Israel was its religion; it was Jewish, not Christian. But in a sense, the new state of Israel was just an extension of the king of the North, who was constantly in conflict with the king of the South, and as it says in verse 14, "… in those times many will rise against the king of the South." With all of this as a backdrop, we now come to verse 15.

> Then the king of the North will come and build up siege ramps and will capture a fortified city. The forces of the South will be powerless to resist; even their best troops will not have the strength to stand. (Daniel 11:15)

This verse is not talking about the newly formed nation of Israel alone because it clearly identifies the king of the North as the aggressor. Verse 15 is actually the introduction of the United States of America who, by the 1960s, has replaced Great Britain to become the biggest defender of the Christian kingdom against Communism and tyranny. The U.S is also the main supporter of Israel, allowing her to exist in the Middle East. By the 1960s, the United States sat atop the greatest empire since Greece under Alexander and Rome. When Britain came to the Middle East in 1917, it kept things in order and allowed many countries to retain their own governments. But by the 1960s, things had changed and the United States became deeply involved in the affairs of the Middle East, assuring the state of Israel of its support. The other big change was oil and the fact that the Middle East had an abundant supply of it. So the U.S. supported Israel on the one hand and on the other hand maintained relations with the Arab world in order to keep the oil flowing. All of this brings us to the Arab-Israeli War of 1967.

The fortified city being talked about in verse 15 is the same city that's been on Daniel's mind all along: Jerusalem. In 1967, Israel became involved in a war known as the "Six-Day War" in which she faced the armies of Egypt, Syria, and Jordan. During that war, Israel captured the Sinai Peninsula, Gaza, the Golan Heights, and the West Bank that included East Jerusalem and the Temple Mount. The Arab nations threw their best at Israel from three directions, but in each case, they suffered defeat. The territory of Israel was much bigger when the conflict was over. But, as verse 16 says, this victory came about because Israel had access to the best military hardware in the world at the time and that support came from the Christian kingdom, or the king of the North: the United States of America and her allies.

The next verse continues to describe the actions of the king of the North:

> The invader will do as he pleases; no one will be able to stand against him. He will establish himself in the Beautiful Land and will have the power to destroy it. He will determine to come with the might of his entire kingdom and will make an alliance with the king of the South. And he will give him a daughter in marriage in order to overthrow the kingdom, but his plans will not succeed or help him. (Daniel 11:16, 17)

As we read this scripture, I would like to take a look at verse 17 in the King James Version because there is a line I find rather interesting: "He shall also set his face to enter with the strength of his whole kingdom, and upright ones with him ..." The Hebrew word for upright is *yashar*, meaning righteous, well pleased, or straight. I believe this refers to the Jewish people who settled in Israel and still reverently kept the law. I believe this scripture is referring to the formation of the state of Israel, which is supported by the king of the North.

Let's take a look at the first part of verse 16: "The invader will do as he pleases; no one will be able to stand against him. He will establish himself in the Beautiful Land and have the power to destroy it." Since 1948, no country has been able to thwart the plans of the king of the North and Israel. Together, they have established themselves, and they have, through nuclear weapons, the power to destroy anything in their path. When has there been any non-Arab power established in "the Beautiful Land?" You'd have to go back to the thirteenth century to see a non-Arab power controlling Jerusalem and the surrounding countryside. The British came in 1917, and subsequently the United States backed the formation of the state of Israel in 1948. Since that time, they have established themselves and no one has been able to stand against them—this scripture can't be talking about anyone else. It's also clearly not the end-time beast power because that's still yet to come in the chapter. This isn't referring to the time of the Crusades because they didn't have the power to permanently establish themselves and they clearly didn't have the power to destroy the Beautiful Land. Furthermore, for those who believe this refers to the time of Antiochus Epiphanies, there was no one who had "the power to destroy it" the way the king of the North and Israel do today. Think about it: neither the Assyrians, Babylonians, Persians, Greeks, Seleucids, Ptolemys, Romans, nor any Arab nation at any time has had the power "to destroy it" the way the king of the North had in 1948–1967 when he occupied the Glorious Land. No one fits this description except the king of the North, who is also described in Daniel Chapter 2 as the ten toes of iron and clay; in Chapter 7 as the fourth beast; and, in this book, as the Christian kingdom. (I left out a comparison to Chapter 8 because it doesn't come into play until verse 18.)

Clearly, on a number of occasions, the king of the North had determined "to come with the might of his entire kingdom." One such time was in 1973 during the Yom-Kippur War when U.S. forces were placed on high alert just in case events got out of hand or the Soviets somehow became involved. President Nixon wanted the world to know, as he told Golda Meier, that the U.S. would stand behind—and defend if needed—the state of Israel.

After that, the U.S., the main power of the North, began to engage in peace talks to form an alliance because they, and others in the kingdom, were beginning to rely more heavily on oil coming out of the king of the South's territory. So on the one hand, the North needed to defend Israel, and on the other, it needed the oil from Israel's adversary. The culmination of this effort occurred with the Camp David peace accords in 1978 where Israel and Egypt agreed to peace, and Israel agreed to give back the Sinai Peninsula. Further peace accords were crafted again between Yitzhak Rabin and Yasser Arafat in 1993. Israel also secured peace with Jordan and to a lesser extent, Syria. Furthermore, the U.S. established solid, peaceful relations with Iran under the shah, still has a friendly business relationship with Saudi Arabia, and had at least a working relationship with Iraq under the pre-Saddam Hussein regime, and got along well with Hussein himself for about ten years. It seemed at that time, the king of the North had established an alliance with the king of the South via peace agreements with Israel, thus assuring that relations between the two kingdoms would be smoother. This is what I believe is talked about in the latter part of verse 17:

> He will determine to come with the might of his entire kingdom and will make an alliance with the king of the South. And he will give him a daughter in marriage in order to overthrow the kingdom, but his plans will not succeed or help him.

The Hebrew word for "overthrow" is *shachath,* which also means to corrupt. In 1978, everything looked good with the alliance between the North and the South; however, that soon ended with the coming Islamic revolution. The last part of verse 17 says the king of the North's plans "will not succeed or help him." The whole peace process between Israel and Egypt, Jordan, Syria, and Saudi Arabia was dealt a blow with the rise of Islamic fundamentalism. The Middle East, which seemed to be achieving more stability after the Camp David accords, was dealt a blow with the fall of Iran to Ayatollah Khomeini. The king of the North had a very hard time dealing with the new Islamic state. Khomeini, a Shiite, also revived the centuries-old conflict between Sunni and Shiite factions. Now, each country's secular government had to deal with the conflict between these two religious groups.

Now let's go to verses 18 and 19 of Daniel 11. This is where events in Chapters 8 and 11 begin to dovetail. From here on, these two chapters describe the same time period and events, but Chapter 11:18–45 gives more detail to complement Chapter 8.

> Then he [the king of the North] will turn his attention to the coastlands and will take many of them, but a commander will put an end to his insolence and will turn his insolence back upon him. After this, he will turn back toward the fortresses of his own country but will stumble and fall, to be seen no more. (Daniel 11:18, 19)

The Hebrew word for coastlands is *iy*—a desirable spot that is coveted or lusted after. The oil-rich countries of the Middle East have become such a spot. Since the late 1970s and '80s the leader of the North, the United States (and to a lesser extent Europe) has become more involved in the eastern part of the Middle East because of the vast supply of oil. In 1990, the North came in and liberated Kuwait from Saddam Hussein. After the conflict was over and Hussein was pushed back to his borders, the United States left a fairly sizable army in Saudi Arabia to protect that country from outside aggression and to make sure the world's largest oil supply continued to flow. The United States also became the military protector of Kuwait and kept a large military force there too. In September 2001, Islamic extremists attacked the United States using commercial airplanes to destroy the World Trade Center. That event provoked the invasion and conquest of Afghanistan in November 2001 and the subsequent invasion and conquest of Iraq in 2003. The U.S. has also maintained a military presence in Qatar and Yemen. Because of oil reserves, these nations have become coveted areas, and as the head of the most powerful nations, the United States has exerted great influence over their affairs.

A similar scenario is discussed in Chapter 8 where a goat kicks down a two-horned ram. The goat is the king of Greece, and the ram's horns represent the kings of Media and Persia. As we discussed in Chapter 4 of this book, the goat represents the Christian kingdom, led by the United States and Great Britain, and the ram represents the areas around Iraq and Iran. The U.S. and Great Britain have already kicked down Iraq, but verse 7 says the goat will furiously strike the ram and shatter his *two* horns. I believe Iran, perhaps along with Syria, will be attacked next. If this is accomplished, the United States, leading the Christian kingdom, will have conquered nearly the same territory conquered by Alexander the Great just before he died.

But the latter part of Daniel 11:18 indicates there will be problems for the king of the North after conquests in the Islamic world. The verse states there will be a "commander," or leader, who will do to them as they have done to others. At this writing, the U.S. is experiencing enormous problems controlling Iraq and Afghanistan because of covert guerrilla war tactics. The "commander" could be someone like Osama Bin Laden of al-Qaeda, or Mahmoud Amadinejad the president of Iran, but eventually this commander causes enough problems (including economic or political problems at home) that the United States decides to vacate a part, or all, of the conquered territories.

Then we get to verse 19 where it says, "... but will stumble and fall, to be seen no more." What could that mean? This same event, I believe, is also described in Daniel 8:8: "The goat became very great, but at the height of his power his large horn was broken off, and in its place four prominent horns grew up toward the four winds of heaven." In verses 21 and 22, it says: "The shaggy goat is the king of Greece, and the large horn between his eyes is the first king. The four horns that replaced the one that was broken off represent four kingdoms that will emerge from his nation but will not have the same power." Some people believe this describes a time when the lead country of the king of the North will cease to exist. Because the Bible doesn't explain exactly what will happen, we can only speculate, but I don't believe the country will disappear completely. I believe these scriptures are all talking about the same event: the fall, or collapse, of the United States as a world power and a decrease in the power of the Western nations.

Large, powerful nations often crumble for the same reason—economics. When I was growing up in the 1960s and 70s, the Soviet Union was an incredible power that was feared by all nations. It seemed by the 1970s that it was inevitable Europe, and maybe the U.S., would be overtaken by the mighty Communist power. In 1980, had someone told me the USSR would collapse by 1991, I would have said they were crazy! There was no way the Soviet Union was going away anytime soon! In fact, when President Reagan used to talk about such a possibility, his staff encouraged former President Nixon to explain to him that that type of thinking wasn't realistic. Nixon tried to tell Reagan, but as he later admitted, he had been wrong and Reagan had been right. Who could have imagined the great Soviet Union would fall? I bring this up because many believe there is no way the United States could ever "stumble and fall." Unfortunately, the history of great empires says otherwise, and the United States may be no different than the British, Spanish, and Dutch who ultimately became second-rate powers because of their precarious financial state. Today, it's not too difficult to see the enormous financial problems that are on the horizon for the United States. The continued loss of manufacturing resulting in a ballooning trade deficit and negative outflow of currency, the continued reliance on foreign oil, and the mounting piles of debt in every aspect of society, all represent enough evidence to make the case that this nation is being weighed down by financial trouble. A great portion of this debt is owned by foreign nations, mostly Japan and China, and if these nations decide to call in the notes or stop buying more debt, there will be big trouble for the United States.

For those who take a clear, close look, I don't believe it's too hard to imagine the United States collapsing for economic reasons. Analysts are bringing up the topic more frequently, banging the drum saying unless there is change in the way individuals and the country run their finances, the future doesn't look so good. There are also other ways this country could be greatly weakened, such as terrorist attacks that cripple the country, or natural disasters that prove too much to handle. The attacks on September 11 and the recent hurricanes and forest fires remind us how vulnerable we are. But at this point, the reason for the king of the North's fall is just speculation. The Bible only says there will be a collapse; it doesn't state the reason why.

The man dressed in linen continues to speak to Daniel:

> His [the king of the North's] successor will send out a tax collector to maintain the royal splendor. In a few years, however, he will be destroyed, yet not in anger or in battle. (Daniel 11:20)

So now we get insight into how the vacuum will be filled when the United States no longer maintains "the royal splendor." Since 1945, the United States, along with the support of Britain, has been the dominant protector of the Christian realm. If the U.S. collapses, someone will need to fill the void. Apparently, it seems it won't be a single country, but an amalgamation of countries—perhaps something like NATO (the North Atlantic Treaty Organization). NATO is, in a sense, a tax collector because it collects revenue and troops from all its members to represent the whole. In fact, as I write (summer 2006), NATO continues to send troops to Afghanistan to replace U.S. troops involved in a conflict that began as a U.S. conflict. So, if the U.S. is greatly reduced in power, it isn't hard to imagine NATO or some similar international body coming together to "maintain the royal splendor." There is also a new configuration that has appeared on the scene in just the last couple of years—the E-3: Britain, France, and Germany. The E-3 represents Europe's three biggest economies and two of its nuclear powers. The E-3 has quickly become a single block that represents most of Europe. They have begun to replace NATO in international negotiations for Europe. This group is the new independent Europe representing itself without the American component involved in NATO. So there are several current groupings of countries that could fill the void left by a destabilized America.

We can again look at Daniel 8:22 to see the same event from a different viewpoint. "The four horns that replaced the one that was broken off represent four kingdoms that will emerge from his nation but will not have the same power." In this case, there is a description of four countries that emerge from the one that has been "broken off." I don't believe America will simply disappear, but I do think it will be severely constricted when it comes to assisting others on the world scene. The U.S. may be one of the four horns that emerge from the one horn that was "broken off." This new configuration won't have the same power it did when the U.S. was the sole leader of the Christian kingdom, and the new group of four won't last very long.

The latter part of Daniel 11:20, 21 tells us the future of the "tax collector":

> His successor will send out a tax collector to maintain the royal splendor. In a few years, however, he will be destroyed, yet not in anger or in battle. He will be succeeded by a contemptible person who has not been given the honor of royalty. He will invade the kingdom when its people feel secure, and he will seize it through intrigue.

The same event is recorded over in Chapter 8, verses 23 and 24:

> In the latter part of their reign [the four horns/tax collector], when rebels have become completely wicked, a stern-faced king, a master of intrigue, will arise. He will become very strong, but not by his own power. He will cause astounding devastation and will succeed in whatever he does.

The same event is also recorded over in Chapter 7, verse 8:

> While I was thinking about the horns, there before me was another horn, a little one, which came up among them; and three of the first horns were

uprooted before it. This horn had eyes like the eyes of a man and a mouth that spoke boastfully.

These verses are all talking about the same thing: the rise of the final ruler. You may have noticed there appears to be a discrepancy with the number of horns in Chapters 7 and 8. Chapter 7 says three will be subdued by the "little horn," and Chapter 8 seems to indicate the stern-faced king subdues four at one time. I believe it's possible the stern-faced king becomes powerful in one nation and then subdues three others. Again, this is speculation because we're dealing with events that have not yet happened, but it's something that bears watching. I think it's better to look at this from a macro view so as to allow for a configuration that may not have been considered.

I have refrained from commenting on other peoples' views of the rise of the final end-time beast, but at this point, I feel the need to comment on a specific issue: the rise of a united Europe as the final end-time beast power. Many people are watching and waiting for Europe to "unite," with the expectation that this unified group of nations will be the little horn with a mouth that speaks boastfully mentioned in Daniel Chapters 7, 8, and 11. There is no direct biblical reference to suggest the "stern-faced king" has to come from Europe. I do believe he has to come from somewhere in the Christian kingdom, which includes the United States, but there is no clear evidence the final beast has to come from Europe—he may, but he may not. The fact that so many (mostly Americans) believe Europe is the place where the beast will come from leads me to think it will probably come from somewhere else, somewhere no one is expecting. We know, from Daniel 8:11 and 11:36, that the little horn will be both government and religion in some way and that he will ultimately want to be worshiped as a god. To produce such an atmosphere, there needs to be a lot of religious fervor, and at this time, Europe is not a place that has a lot of religious zeal, or a place that mixes religion and government together. In fact, Europe has become a fairly secular continent, although things can always change. The United States, on the other hand, is a place with a highly charged religious element that quite often wants to put religion and government together. It's no secret that the current president, George W. Bush, drew enormous support from those who identified themselves as religious. I know of people who believed that voting for George Bush was like voting for "God's side." I bring all of this up because you can make a pretty good case that the "little horn" might come from the United States. Again, I'm not saying this will definitely happen; I'm saying that because there are no scriptures stating exactly where this little horn will come from, we should keep an open mind to the possibility that it could come from any nation within the Christian kingdom.

As we read through Chapter 11 verses 21 through 45, we come to the final ruler of the kingdom of the North, the ruler that leads the Christian kingdom up until the time that Jesus Christ returns, destroys the kingdoms of man, and sets up His own everlasting kingdom. The focus is entirely on this "contemptible person," who is also the "little horn," and the "stern-faced master of intrigue." All three appellations are the same person, or government. These verses describe in detail what Daniel wanted to know back in Chapter 7, verse 20: "I also wanted to know about the ten horns on its head and about the other horn that came up, before which three of them fell—the horn that looked more imposing than the others and that had eyes and a mouth that spoke boastfully." Since we don't know exactly who this is, we will look at the following verses in a way that gives us a framework of events so that when we see certain situations occurring on the world scene, we will recognize where they align with what is written in the Bible.

The structure of these next twenty-four verses isn't set up in chronological order. Instead, as is sometimes the case throughout the Bible, several verses cover the overview of an event, and then immediately in the following verses, the event is retold, but with the emphasis on a specific action. The passage may read as though an event is happening twice, but in fact, it's the same event with a different focus. For example, in this case, verses 21–24 describe the entire reign of the "contemptible person"; verses 25–28 describe the king of the South waging war against the king of the North and losing many of his people in battle, and then the king of the North beginning to persecute the people of the holy covenant; verses 29–35 describe the final invasion of the king of the South's kingdom and the fullness of the persecution; verses 36–39 describe the religious actions of the king of the North; and finally verses 40–45 again describe the final invasion, the king of the North's accomplishments, countries that will escape being conquered by him, the coming forces from Asia, the intense persecution of the saints, and the king of the North's end on Mount Moriah. All of this may seem somewhat confusing, but it's my hope the scriptures will become much clearer as we go through these verses sequentially and explain in more detail the events being described.

So now let's go back to Daniel 11:21:

> He [the tax collector] will be succeeded by a contemptible person who has not been given the honor of royalty. He will invade the kingdom when its people feel secure, and he will seize it through intrigue. Then an overwhelming army

will be swept away before him; both it and a prince of the covenant will be destroyed. After coming to an agreement with him, he will act deceitfully, and with only a few people he will rise to power. When the richest provinces feel secure, he will invade them and will achieve what neither his fathers nor his forefathers did. He will distribute plunder, loot and wealth among his followers. He will plot the overthrow of fortresses—but only for a time. (Daniel 11:21–24)

I can't help thinking this is some kind of military person who assists the leaders of the Christian kingdom and through "intrigue," or deception, arranges a backdoor coup to eventually seize power. There is no proof of this, but when you look back through history, these kinds of events usually involve someone with military standing. It appears this person arranges the destruction of any military opposition so as to secure his power. With his newly found power, he attacks and a great army is defeated. Verse 22 says the great army *and* "a prince of the covenant" are destroyed. The Hebrew word for "prince" is *nagid*, which means military or religious leader; the Living Bible uses "the leader of priests" for the phrase "prince of the covenant." I believe this verse is talking about the destruction of a religious leader, group, or country. The term "covenant" as used in this chapter refers to a pact between God and His people, and this entire vision is about "what will happen to your people in the future," so this very well could be referring to Jews/Israel or those who follow Christ, or both. This occurs, as we find out later in the chapter, because the "contemptible person" is moving government and religion into one entity, and he ultimately wants to be worshiped. Those who keep the covenant most likely refuse to comply. There are companion scriptures in Daniel Chapters 7 and 8, as well as Revelation 13, that talk about this same event—the destruction of "the mighty men and holy people." It seems this person is conflating power to himself because of a financial and/or military proposition that makes people feel it's beneficial to cede power to this one man to provide more strength in a central power structure. Once he has power, he uses it to conquer others and expand his dominion. He then promises the masses that support him prosperity through redistribution of the riches he has taken.

What does it mean when it says, "[he] ... will achieve what neither his fathers nor his forefathers did"? It doesn't seem like this is talking about land conquests, because the Christian kingdom has on a few occasions been pretty closely united. In 1945, for example, the United States controlled the entire Christian kingdom; in fact, the U.S. controlled most of the world, so I don't think that's what's being talked about here. I think this verse is talking about combining government and religion into one, something that hasn't happened in the Christian kingdom for a long time, although some have tried. Not since the Roman emperors has there been a major European theocracy, and America has never seen such a condition. For the last 1800 or so years, Europe and America have kept government and religion separate, although religion involved itself many times in government affairs. However, the apex of this coming power will be marked by something that has never been done: ruling the Christian kingdom by theocracy. Furthermore, the leader of this theocracy will not just be government and religion rolled into one; he also wants to be worshiped as divine. Sound strange? It sure does, but it's what has been forecasted in Daniel and other places in the Bible. I'll talk more about this when we cover verses 36–39. The point to remember is that worship is going to be the most important issue; this final power will want to be worshiped more than anything else.

This "contemptible person" will have grand designs to conquer many places and be worshiped as god, but then, at the appointed time, he will meet his end. One of the "fortresses" he will plot to overthrow will be the Temple Mount, one of the most revered religious sites in the world. It will be at the Temple Mount in Jerusalem that he sets up his place of self-worship, and it will be from there that he'll meet his end at the appointed time.

Verse 25 brings us back to the early parts of the contemptible person's rule where he is preparing his Christian kingdom for war against the Islamic nations, or the king of the South:

> With a large army he will stir up his strength and courage against the king of the South. The king of the South will wage war with a large and very powerful army, but he will not be able to stand because of the plots devised against him. Those who eat from the king's provisions will try to destroy him; his army will be swept away, and many will fall in battle. The two kings, with their hearts bent on evil, will sit at the same table and lie to each other, but to no avail, because an end will still come at the appointed time. The king of the North will return to his own country with great wealth, but his heart will be set against the holy covenant. He will take action against it and then return to his own country. (Daniel 11:25–28)

The whole concept of stirring up strength and courage against the king of the South isn't difficult to imagine in today's political atmosphere. The Christian nations use the terms "terror" and "terrorism" to whip up nationalistic sentiment against Islamic countries such as Iraq, Iran, and Syria. The atmosphere is so charged with emotion that most of the Christian kingdom is pitted against most of the Islamic countries in the Middle East. Verse 25 seems to indicate that the king of the North, sensing opportunity or danger, engages the king of the South in battle, and the southern kingdom suffers a huge defeat. The king of the North is clearly victorious because he is the one who returns to his country with great wealth, and these verses say the king of the South will be weakened because of internal disagreements. However, according to verse 27, there will be some kind of a peace conference between the two sides to negotiate a conclusion to the hostilities, but the motives on both sides will be insincere and disingenuous. Verse 28 says the king of the North's "heart will be set against the holy covenant. He will take action against it ..." It's clear that something will occur that begins religious persecution, and the king of the North is involved in it away from his country, most likely when he is in the Middle East.

The next verse, verse 29, begins with the phrase "at the appointed time," which means the time of the very end, the last phase. This is also the same event described in verse 40, which begins, "At the time of the end ..." So we'll look at these verses together—verses 29–39 and 40–45—and see what each section adds to the overall picture of the time right before the return of Jesus Christ. As we begin, the king of the North makes a final assault against the king of the South:

> At the appointed time he will invade the South again, but this time the outcome will be different from what it was before. Ships of the western coastlands [of Kittim] will oppose him, and he will lose heart. Then he will turn back and vent his fury against the holy covenant. He will return and show favor to those who forsake the holy covenant. (Daniel 11:29, 30a)

This corresponds to verses 40–44:

> At the time of the end the king of the South will engage him in battle, and the king of the North will storm out against him with chariots and cavalry and a great fleet of ships. He will invade many countries and sweep through them like a flood. He will also invade the Beautiful Land. Many countries will fall, but Edom, Moab, and the leaders of Ammon will be delivered from his hand. He will extend his power over many countries; Egypt will not escape. He will gain control of the treasures of gold and silver and all the riches of Egypt, with the Libyans and Nubians in submission. But reports from the east and the north will alarm him, and he will set out in a great rage to destroy and annihilate many. (Daniel 11:40–45)

Both accounts begin with a battle between the king of the North and the king of the South. But this time, the outcome is different than in the previous battle where the king of the South's army was swept away, because the king of the

North has problems with ships from the western coastlands and reports from the east and north. How can these verses be describing the same event? In both cases, the North invades the South and then becomes alarmed. The "western coast-lands," or *Kittim* in Hebrew, describes the land of Cyprus as being the place of opposition, and it's quite obvious that the navy on the tiny island of Cyprus is not the force that's going cause the king to lose heart. If a naval force is in fact the opposition to the North, there are only a few countries with such power. Since the U.S., Britain, and Europe are part of the Northern kingdom, their navies are part of the "great fleet of ships" that invade the South, so they can't be part of the opposition. This leaves only two other countries with established blue-water navies: Russia and China. China's navy right now is growing at such a rate that many believe it will be equal to the U.S. Navy in capability in the not-too-distant future. Russia and China, along with India, are east and north of the "Beautiful Land" and would certainly qualify as countries that could alarm, or concern, the leader of the Christian kingdom who has invaded and gained control of the coun-tries of the Middle East and northern Africa. It's no secret that China now relies on oil from the Middle East as much, if not more, than the U.S. and would be greatly concerned if the flow of oil were somehow interrupted. As of this writing, China is expected to exceed the U.S.'s oil consumption within three years. China, Russia, and India combined equal half the world's population—a sizable force to be reckoned with. With this scenario, the Christian kingdom would be fighting the Islamic kingdom, and then the major countries of Asia would become involved—all of the world's major armies would be in conflict in the Middle East. This will happen only once, at the time of the end. This is how we know verses 29–30 and 40–44 are describing the same event.

The statement in verse 41, "He will also invade the Beautiful Land" brings up an interesting question: Why does the king of the North have to invade the Beau-tiful Land? We know from reading verses 14–16 the king of the North establishes himself there, and there is no written account of him losing the area. What hap-pens in the interim? There are two possibilities worth considering. One is that the king of the North cedes the land, the state of Israel, to the king of the South in some kind of peace deal or other action when the kings of the North and South negotiate with each other ("The two kings … will sit at the same table and lie to each other …"), although at this writing, this scenario seems unlikely. The other possibility is that the king of the North becomes upset with the state of Israel for some reason and decides to take it over. The reasons for such an action could cen-ter on religion, politics, or even military power, but verse 41 clearly indicates an invasion of the state of Israel by the Christian kingdom.

Another interesting point in verse 41 is the list of countries—Edom, Ammon, and Moab—who escape the "hand" of the invader. Why do these countries escape, and who are they? Edom and Ammon are possibly Turkey and Jordan (the capital of Jordan is Ammon), and the reason they escape may be due to their close relationship with the Christian kingdom. At this writing, Turkey is a member of NATO and a candidate for EU membership, so it's possible this trend of friendship will continue into the final end-time invasion of the Islamic kingdom.

So the stage has been set. The king of the North has invaded and controls much of the kingdom of the South, including Israel that is under military occupation. He is alarmed at what he hears from the north and east and turns his attention to their approaching armies. What happens next is shocking for the people of God, but it is also one of the reasons why God gives prophecy. Daniel 11:30–39 says:

> Ships of the western coastlands will oppose him, and he will lose heart. Then he will turn back and vent his fury against the holy covenant. He will return and show favor to those who forsake the holy covenant.
>
> His armed forces will rise up to desecrate the temple fortress and will abolish the daily sacrifice. Then they will set up the abomination that causes desolation. With flattery he will corrupt those who have violated the covenant, but the people who know their God will firmly resist him.
>
> Those who are wise will instruct many, though for a time they will fall by the sword or be burned or captured or plundered. When they fall, they will receive a little help, and many who are not sincere will join them. Some of the wise will stumble, so that they may be refined, purified and made spotless until the time of the end, for it will still come at the appointed time.

A period of terrible persecution of the people of the holy covenant is prophesied to come at the end of the age. Who are the people of the holy covenant? They are the people who know who God is and worship only Him; they don't worship the king who will "exalt and magnify himself above every god ..." They worship God the way He wants to be worshiped—through obedience to His prescribed way of life. This takes us full circle back to the beginning of the book of Daniel where we saw how God's people responded to life-threatening decrees of kings who didn't know the true God. As Shadrach, Meshach, and Abednego said: "O Nebuchadnezzar, we do not need to defend ourselves before you in this matter. If we are thrown into the blazing furnace, the God we serve is able to save us from it, and he will rescue us from your hand, O king. But even if he does not, we want you to know, O king, that we will not serve your gods or worship the image of gold you have set up." God responded by saving the lives of the three men, but Daniel 11 says during this time of trouble at the end of the age, God's people will be killed or taken captive. But the outcome is sure—those who worship God are under a covenant where they will ultimately be blessed to inherit eternal life in the kingdom of God.

◆   ◆   ◆

Somewhere around 2000 BC, a father and his only son, the result of a miraculous promise, stopped on the top of a mountain after a three-day journey to worship God. Their God had commanded a sacrifice from the father to show his obedience. The offering was the man's beloved son. As they reached the top of the mountain, the father and son built an altar and stacked the wood neatly for burning. The father bound his son and laid him carefully on top of the wood, then with his arm up in the air, he gripped the handle of his knife and prepared to slit the throat of his son. Suddenly, an angel called out:

> "Abraham! Abraham!"
> "Here I am," he replied.
> "Do not lay a hand on the boy," he said. "Do not do anything to him. Now I know that you fear God, because you have not withheld from me your son, your only son."

Flooded with relief, the father put down the knife, and when he looked up, he found a ram caught in a nearby bush. With great joy, Abraham offered the ram as an offering to God. The boy who was spared that day was Isaac, Abraham's son, the one through whom Jesus Christ would come nearly 2,000 years later. Abraham, in thanks and celebration, gave a name to the mountain where this event took place: "So Abraham called that place The Lord Will Provide. And to this day it is said, 'On the mountain of the Lord it will be provided'" (Genesis 22:11–14). Today, the name of that mountain is Mount Moriah. This was where God placed His name after David bought the threshing floor from Araunah the Jebusite, where King Solomon built the temple, and where Israel offered sacrifices to God. It is the very same place God sacrificed His only Son, the Son of a miraculous promise, the Lamb of God known as Jesus Christ, to fulfill His promise to Abraham that "through your offspring all nations on earth will be blessed, because you have obeyed me." Because Jesus died and was resurrected, we now have the hope of resurrection to eternal life. This same mountain, Mount Moriah, will be the central location for the last major event of the age, the place where the end-time king, the little horn with eyes and a mouth that speaks boastfully, will set up *his* temple as a place where he is worshiped as a god.

> His armed forces will rise up to desecrate the temple fortress and will abolish the daily sacrifice. Then they will set up the abomination that causes desolation. With flattery he will corrupt those who have violated the covenant, but the people who know their God will firmly resist him. (Daniel 11:31, 32)

> The king will do as he pleases. He will exalt and magnify himself above every god and will say unheard-of things against the God of gods. He will be successful until the time of the wrath is completed, for what has been determined must take place. (Verse 36)

We can compare this to Matthew 24 to see what Jesus Christ had to say about this very event. His disciples had asked Him about the end of the age. "'Tell us,' they said, 'when will this happen, and what will be the sign of your coming and of the end of the age?'" Interestingly, the conversation took place on the Mount of Olives, an area that looks across to Mount Moriah—the very location where Christ ascended into heaven and where He will return to establish His kingdom.

> Then you will be handed over to be persecuted and put to death, and you will be hated by all nations because of me. At that time many will turn away from the faith and will betray and hate each other, and many false prophets will appear and deceive many people. Because of the increase of wickedness, the love of most will grow cold, but he who stands firm to the end will be saved. And this gospel of the kingdom will be preached in the whole world as a testimony to all nations, and then the end will come.
> So when you see standing in the holy place "the abomination that causes desolation," spoken of through the prophet Daniel—let the reader understand … (Matthew 24:9–15)

In II Thessalonians 2:3, 4, the apostle Paul says: "Don't let anyone deceive you in any way, for that day will not come until the rebellion occurs and the man of lawlessness is revealed, the man doomed to destruction. He will oppose and will exalt himself over everything that is called God or is worshiped, so that he sets himself up in God's temple, proclaiming himself to be God."

All of these scriptures warn of the same event at the end of the age—a man who sets himself up in God's place and demands worship, persecuting those who faithfully worship the true God.

As we previously mentioned back in Chapter 6 of this book, the desecration of the temple fortress and abolishing of the daily sacrifices is symbolic of the destruction of God's people. The next few verses describe the terrifying time of the end when the saints go through what is known as the great tribulation.

> Those who are wise [the people of God] will instruct many, though for a time they will fall by the sword or be burned or be captured or plundered. When they fall, they will receive a little help, and many who are not sincere will join them. Some of the wise will stumble, so that they may be refined, purified and made spotless until the time of the end, for it will still come at the appointed time. (Daniel 11:33–35)

There is so much information about the end time in these three short verses. This passage seems to mention three distinct groups. First, the wise who "receive a little help" do so as they "fall." In other words, they are being persecuted and martyred, and as this happens, they receive help in some way from God, but it doesn't seem to refer to a rapture. This might be a good time to look at what I believe is a parallel account over in the book of Revelation. In Revelation 3:7–13, Jesus Christ is talking to a church that appears to be around at the end of the age:

> "To the angel of the church in Philadelphia write:
> These are the words of him who is holy and true, who holds the key of David. What he opens no one can shut, and what he shuts no one can open. I know your deeds. See, I have placed before you an open door that no one can shut. I know that you have little strength, yet you have kept my word and have not denied my name. I will make those who are of the synagogue of Satan, who claim to be Jews though they are not, but are liars—I will make them come and fall down at your feet and acknowledge that I have loved you. Since you have kept my command to endure patiently, I will also keep you from the hour of trial that is going to come upon the whole world to test those who live on the earth.
> I am coming soon. Hold on to what you have, so that no one will take your crown. Him who overcomes I will make a pillar in the temple of my God. Never again will he leave it. I will write on him the name of my God and the name of the city of my God, the new Jerusalem, which is coming down out of heaven from my God; and I will also write on him my new name. He who has an ear, let him hear what the Spirit says to the churches.

There is also the account in Revelation 13:5–10 that speaks of an end-time ruler and how he deals with God's people:

The beast was given a mouth to utter proud words and blasphemies and to exercise his authority for forty-two months. He opened his mouth to blaspheme God, and to slander his name and his dwelling place and those who live in heaven. He was given power to make war against the saints and to conquer them. And he was given authority over every tribe, people, language and nation. All inhabitants of the earth will worship the beast—all whose names have not been written in the book of life belonging to the Lamb that was slain from the creation of the world.

He who has an ear, let him hear.

If anyone is to go into captivity, into captivity he will go. If anyone is to be killed with the sword, with the sword he will be killed.

This calls for patient endurance and faithfulness on the part of the saints.

This is a parallel description of what's written in Daniel 7:25 and 8:12, 24. All of these scriptures support an end-time persecution of the saints; there doesn't seem to be discussion of a rapture.

The assurance of a little help doesn't necessarily promise protection from death. A biblical example of something similar happening is when Stephen was stoned to death: "When they heard this, they were furious and gnashed their teeth at him. But Stephen, full of the Holy Spirit, looked up to heaven and saw the glory of God, and Jesus standing at the right hand of God. 'Look,' he said, 'I see heaven open and the Son of Man standing at the right hand of God.' At this they covered their ears and, yelling at the top of their voices, they all rushed at him, dragged him out of the city and began to stone him … While they were stoning him, Stephen prayed, 'Lord Jesus, receive my spirit.' Then he fell on his knees and cried out, 'Lord, do not hold this sin against them.' When he had said this, he fell asleep" (Acts 7:54–60). The sight of the glory of God greatly encouraged and strengthened Stephen, and that would certainly qualify as "a little help." When the scripture refers to keeping "you from the hour of trial that is going to come upon the whole world to test those who live on the earth," we shouldn't read this as a rapture. The Bible is filled with accounts of people who worshiped God and died in service to Him. What receiving "a little help" means is still speculative, but it doesn't seem to refer to a rapture because these people still die.

The second group mentioned is an unusual group: "many who are not sincere will join them." Since we only have this one description, it's difficult to say exactly who this group is. It seems that they are not part of the "wise"—those who know their God. There is a description of a great multitude of people in Revelation 7:9, 10 (listed after the 144,000 "servants of our God" are sealed):

After this I looked and there before me was a great multitude that no one could count, from every nation, tribe, people and language, standing before the throne and in front of the Lamb. They were wearing white robes and were holding palm branches in their hands. And they cried out in a loud voice: "Salvation belongs to our God, who sits on the throne, and to the Lamb."

Verses 13–17 say:

Then one of the elders asked me, "These in white robes—who are they, and where did they come from?"

I answered, "Sire, you know."

And he said, "These are they who have come out of the great tribulation; they have washed their robes and made them white in the blood of the Lamb. Therefore,

"they are before the throne of God and serve him day and night in his temple; and he who sits on the throne will spread his tent over them. Never again will they hunger; never again will they thirst. The sun will not beat upon them, nor any scorching heat. For the Lamb at the center of the throne will be their shepherd; he will lead them to springs of living water. And God will wipe away every tear from their eyes."

This might be describing the second group. It's also possible that "many who are not sincere" are part of the third group—the wise who stumble—who seem to be described in Revelation 3:14–21 (see below). From the short phrase in Daniel 11, we don't know in what way this insincere group will join the wise—by instructing many? By resisting the king of the North? By dying in the end time? When we aren't sure of an answer in the Bible, all we can do is be aware of the scriptures and keep an open mind. When we need to know who or what something is, God will reveal it.

The third group seems to be described in the message from Jesus Christ to the Laodicean church:

"To the angel of the church of Laodicea write:

These are the words of the Amen, the faithful and true witness, the ruler of God's creation. I know your deeds, that you are neither cold nor hot. I wish you were either one or the other! So, because you are lukewarm—neither hot nor cold—I am about to spit you out of my mouth. You say, 'I am rich; I have acquired wealth and do not need a thing.' But you do not realize that you are wretched, pitiful, poor, blind and naked. I counsel you to buy from me gold refined in the fire, so you can become rich; and white clothes to wear, so you can cover your shameful nakedness; and salve to put on your eyes, so you can see. Those whom I love I rebuke and discipline. So be earnest, and repent ..."

This is close to the same terminology used in Daniel 11:35 and seems to be the clearest description of the three groups. This group is called by God, but they fall short and must go through some type of martyrdom so that they may be made righteous. As Jesus said, "If anyone would come after me, he must deny himself and take up his cross and follow me. For whoever wants to save his life will lose it, but whoever loses his life for me and for the gospel will save it" (Mark 8:34, 35).

Both churches—the church in Philadelphia and the church in Laodicea—refer to God's people at the end time. These are saints who are present during the time in which the "little horn" rules and sets up worship, and they all experience a tremendous persecution. In Revelation 1:20, the resurrected Jesus says to John, "The mystery of the seven stars that you saw in my right hand and of the seven golden lampstands is this: The seven stars are the angels of the seven churches, and the seven lampstands are the seven churches." In Chapter 11, two of the seven churches are told to prophesy:

"... And I will give power to my two witnesses, and they will prophesy for 1,260 days, clothed in sackcloth." These are the two olive trees and the two lampstands that stand before the Lord of the earth. If anyone tries to harm them, fire comes from their mouths and devours their enemies. This is how anyone who wants to harm them must die. These men have power to shut up the sky so that it will not rain during the time they are prophesying; and they have power to turn the waters into blood and to strike the earth with every kind of plague as often as they want.

Now when they have finished their testimony, the beast that comes up from the Abyss will attack them, and overpower and kill them. Their bodies will lie in the street of the great city, which is figuratively called Sodom and Egypt, where also their Lord was crucified. For three and a half days men from every people, tribe, language and nation will gaze on their bodies and refuse them burial ... But after the three and a half days a breath of life from God entered them, and they stood on their feet, and terror struck those who saw them. Then they heard a loud voice from heaven saying to them, "Come up here." And they went up to heaven in a cloud, while their enemies looked on. (Revelation 11:3–12)

These scriptures suggest a persecution for the people who worship God at the end of the age, not an early rapture.

Now we go back to the description of the "contemptible person" in Daniel 11. This is the same ruler mentioned in Chapter 7, "This horn had eyes like the eyes of a man and a mouth that spoke boastfully," and Chapter 8 "a stern-faced king, a master of intrigue." This is the last description in the book of Daniel of this final king of the North.

> The king will do as he pleases. He will exalt and magnify himself above every god and will say unheard-of things against the God of gods. He will be successful until the time of wrath is completed, for what has been determined must take place.

There are so many rulers and kings throughout history who became despotic and deluded with power, believing they were almost divine and deserving of worship. But apparently, this end-time individual is somehow different and far more destructive. Throughout Daniel, there are indications that this king derives his power from behind-the-scenes spiritual forces (Satan) and that power has been restrained by God but will be unleashed at the appointed time. Jesus Christ, in Matthew 24, talks about the great deception that will occur during this time: "At that time if anyone says to you, 'Look, here is the Christ!' or, 'There he is!' do not believe it. For false Christs and false prophets will appear and perform great signs and miracles to deceive even the elect—if that were possible. See, I have told you ahead of time" (Verses 23–25). However, the good news is that it is not possible to deceive the elect because they have been sealed with the Holy Spirit, and as it says in Daniel 11:32, "… but the people who know their God will firmly resist him [the contemptible person]." So apparently, many will give this final beast power what he wants most—worship—but the "wise" will know he is a deceitful fraud and won't worship him, even if it means their death.

All of this will happen during what is known as "the time of wrath," and its duration is completely under God's control. In fact, Christ said the time was going to be cut short for the sake of the saints. This final beast power will be successful only because God allows it.

We learn more about the contemptible person in verse 37:

> He will show no regard for the gods of his fathers or for the one desired by women, nor will he regard any god, but will exalt himself above them all. Instead of them, he will honor a god of fortresses; a god unknown to his fathers he will honor with gold and silver, with precious stones and costly gifts.

This king raises himself above what is being worshiped now. He institutes something new that's not known to the churches of the Christian kingdom, and it especially affects the leader of those churches—Catholicism. There is a great deal of discussion in Revelation 17 and 18 about a large religious system, or church, being destroyed by this very king who exalts himself. This is probably what is meant when it refers to him showing no regard for the gods of his fathers or the one desired by women. This new worship system may revert back to direct Mithra worship, or some form of worship of the Zoroastrian pantheon. It's hard to know for sure, but it's something to watch for as we move into the future. This contemptible person will gain followers because, as verse 39 states: "He will attack the mightiest fortresses with the help of a foreign god and will greatly honor those who acknowledge him. He will make them rulers over many people and will distribute the land at a price." The fortresses will probably include Mount Moriah in Jerusalem. People will think this is a good thing and won't recognize that it's all a deception to follow and worship Satan. This king will pitch "his royal tents between the seas at the beautiful holy mountain." Then what?

"At the Appointed Time"

Daniel is told in Chapter 11 that the end of the age is *inevitable*: "… because an end will still come at the appointed time" (verse 27) and "… the time of the end, for it will still come at the appointed time" (verse 35). I don't think words on paper can express what that really means—the end of this age and the beginning of the next age when God sets up His kingdom and rules forever! As it says in Daniel 2:44: "In the time of those kings, the God of heaven will set up a kingdom that will never be destroyed, nor will it be left to another people. It will crush all those kingdoms and bring them to an end, but it will itself endure forever." Chapter 7:13, 14 says: "In my vision at night I looked, and there before me was one like a son of man, coming with the clouds of heaven. He approached the Ancient of Days and was led into his presence. He was given authority, glory and sovereign power; all peoples, nations and men of every language worshiped him. His dominion is an everlasting dominion that will not pass away, and his kingdom is one that will never be destroyed." It will be like nothing we humans have ever known or experienced.

You would think the world would rejoice at this climactic event, but we are told the world mourns at the coming of the Son of Man: "At that time the sign of the Son of man will appear in the sky, and all the nations of the earth will mourn. They will see the Son of Man coming on the clouds of the sky, with power and great glory" (Matthew 24:30).

Daniel 12 continues the message from the man dressed in linen:

> At that time Michael, the great prince who protects your people, will arise. There will be a time of distress such as has not happened from the beginning of nations until then. But at that time your people—everyone whose name is found written in the book—will be delivered. Multitudes who sleep in the dust of the earth will awake: some to everlasting life, others to shame and everlasting contempt. Those who are wise will shine like the brightness of the heavens, and those who lead many to righteousness, like the stars for ever and ever. (Daniel 12:1–3)

Again, the archangel Michael is active, but this time, it's at the end of the age. This passage gives us more information on who Daniel's people are: those whose names are "found written in the book." And the first question the reader asks is, "What book?" In Psalm 69:28, King David asks that his enemies "... be blotted out of the book of life and not be listed with the righteous." In the book of Philippians, Paul says "... help these women who have contended at my side in the cause of the gospel, along with Clement and the rest of my fellow workers, whose names are in the book of life." There are several passages in the book of Revelation that refer to this same book. "He who overcomes will, like them, be dressed in white. I will never blot out his name from the book of life, but will acknowledge his name before my Father and his angels" (3:5). "All inhabitants of the earth will worship the beast—all whose names have not been written in the book of life belonging to the Lamb that was slain from the creation of the world" (13:8). "The beast, which you saw, once was, now is not, and will come up out of the Abyss and go to his destruction. The inhabitants of the earth whose names have not been written in the book of life from the creation of the world will be astonished when they see the beast, because he once was, now is not, and yet will come" (17:8). "And I saw the dead, great and small, standing before the throne, and books were opened. Another book was opened, which is the book of life. The dead were judged according to what they had done as recorded in the books ... If anyone's name was not found written in the book of life, he was thrown into the lake of fire" (20:12, 15). Describing "the Holy City, the new Jerusalem, coming down out of heaven from God ..." (21:2), John says, "Nothing impure will ever enter it, nor will anyone who does what is shameful or deceitful, but only those whose names are written in the Lamb's book of life" (21:27). These passages tell us the people who are in the book of life are those who are righteous—those who worship God. Those who are not found written in the book of life are those who choose not to worship God, and they'll be destroyed. The man dressed in linen refers to Daniel's people as "everyone whose name is found written in the book." "At that time"—the time of the end—Daniel's people are the righteous who worship God.

Multitudes Who Sleep in the Dust

This passage in Daniel also speaks of a great resurrection! "Multitudes who sleep in the dust of the earth will awake: some to everlasting life, others to shame and everlasting contempt." There is a lot of confusion about what happens to people after they die. Some people believe that when you die, you go to heaven or hell;

some believe there is an intermediary state where you wait for a certain amount of time to go by before you reach some type of resolution; some believe you come back to life as something else; and I'm sure there are many more ideas. It would probably surprise most people to learn that God is quite clear on what happens after death. The Bible teaches that *all* people who have died are still in the ground awaiting resurrection. The Bible often refers to people who have died as "sleeping." In John 11:11–15, Jesus tells His disciples,

> "Our friend Lazarus has fallen asleep; but I am going there to wake him up."
> His disciples replied, "Lord, if he sleeps, he will get better." Jesus had been speaking of his death, but his disciples thought he meant natural sleep.
> So then he told them plainly, "Lazarus is dead, and for your sake I am glad I was not there, so that you may believe. But let us go to him.'"

Jesus Christ, who was God, miraculously went through this process of death and resurrection Himself. In Matthew 12:40, He says, "For as Jonah was three days and three nights in the belly of a huge fish, so the Son of Man will be three days and three nights in the heart of the earth." Jesus was asleep in the earth for three days and three nights—He was dead! Many mistakenly believe He went straight to heaven, but if that were so, why would He say to Mary, after being resurrected, "Do not hold on to me, for I have not yet returned to the Father. Go instead to my brothers and tell them, 'I am returning to my Father and your Father, to my God and your God'" (John 20:17). Jesus completed the cycle of human life: He was born; He lived a physical life (although He did it without sinning); He died and was buried in the ground; and three days and three nights later, He was resurrected to eternal life by the Father. He tasted death for us. We will go through the same process of birth, life, death, and resurrection, but some will be resurrected to eternal life, while others will be resurrected to shame and everlasting contempt. It all depends on whether or not your name is written in the book of life.

As it says in Ecclesiastes 9:5, 6: "For the living know that they will die, but the dead know nothing; they have no further reward, and even the memory of them is forgotten. Their love, their hate and their jealousy have long since vanished; never again will they have a part in anything that happens under the sun." This doesn't describe any kind of afterlife. Regarding the resurrection, in the book of Ezekiel, the entire thirty-seventh chapter is devoted to describing the resurrection—the dead being brought back to life:

The hand of the Lord was upon me, and he brought me out by the Spirit of the Lord and set me in the middle of a valley; it was full of bones. He led me back and forth among them, and I saw a great many bones on the floor of the valley, bones that were very dry. He asked me, "Son of man, can these bones live?"

I said, "O Sovereign Lord, you alone know."

Then he said to me, "Prophecy to these bones and say to them, 'Dry bones, hear the word of the Lord! This is what the Sovereign Lord says to these bones. I will make breath enter you, and you will come to life. I will attach tendons to you and make flesh come upon you and cover you with skin; I will put breath in you, and you will come to life. Then you will know that I am the Lord." (Verses 1–6)

Then he said to me: "Son of man, these bones are the whole house of Israel. They say, 'Our bones are dried up and our hope is gone; we are cut off.' Therefore prophesy and say this to them: 'This is what the Sovereign Lord says: O my people, I am going to open your graves and bring you up from them; I will bring you back to the land of Israel. Then you, my people, will know that I am the Lord, when I open your graves and bring you up from them. I will put my Spirit in you and you will live, and I will settle you in your own land. Then you will know that I the Lord have spoken, and I have done it, declares the Lord.'" (Verses 11–14)

There is no discussion of another state of existence. Those who have died are simply dead in the ground without life, knowledge, feeling, or awareness. Some people argue this refers to those who died under the old covenant, but now that Christ has been resurrected from the dead, the gates of heaven are open and many are allowed to enter. Let's look at what the apostle Peter said after the death and resurrection of Jesus Christ. Peter gives his famous sermon on the day of Pentecost, one of God's holy days listed in Leviticus 23. In Acts 2:29–31, 34, he refers to King David: "Brothers, I can tell you confidently that the patriarch David died and was buried, and his tomb is here to this day. But he was a prophet and knew that God had promised him on oath that he would place one of his descendants on his throne. Seeing what was ahead, he spoke of the resurrection of the Christ, that he was not abandoned to the grave, nor did his body see decay … For David did not ascend to heaven …" Peter makes it quite clear that King David is still in the grave, not in heaven, but he did speak of Jesus Christ's death and resurrection. So we see that Jesus has been resurrected, but everyone else who has died is awaiting the resurrection at the appointed time.

It was because of Paul's belief in the resurrection that many hated him, and it was the reason he was arrested. Paul had been brought before the Sanhedrin, a religious council comprised of Pharisees and Sadducees. "Then Paul, knowing that some of them were Sadducees and the others Pharisees, called out in the Sanhedrin, 'My brothers, I am a Pharisee, the son of a Pharisee. I stand on trial because of my hope in the resurrection of the dead.' When he said this, a dispute broke out between the Pharisees and the Sadducees, and the assembly was divided. (The Sadducees say that there is no resurrection, and that there are neither angels nor spirits, but the Pharisees acknowledge them all)" (Acts 23:6–8). Paul went on to explain to Governor Felix why he was arrested and put on trial: "But there are some Jews from the province of Asia, who ought to be here before you and bring charges if they have anything against me. Or these who are here should state what crime they found in me when I stood before the Sanhedrin—unless it was this one thing I shouted as I stood in their presence: 'It is concerning the resurrection of the dead that I am on trial before you today'" (Acts 24:19–21). And finally, Paul summed up the whole point when he appeared before King Agrippa: "And now it is because of my hope in what God has promised our fathers that I am on trial today. This is the promise our twelve tribes are hoping to see fulfilled as they earnestly serve God day and night. O king, it is because of this hope that the Jews are accusing me. Why should any of you consider it incredible that God raises the dead?" (Acts 26:6–8).

As Paul explains, the resurrection of the dead is at the very core of Christian faith; without it, there is no hope for mankind. In I Corinthians 15, the apostle Paul's focus is entirely on what happens after death. Picking up Paul's thoughts in verse 12:

> But if it is preached that Christ has been raised from the dead, how can some of you say that there is no resurrection of the dead? If there is no resurrection of the dead, then not even Christ has been raised. And if Christ has not been raised, our preaching is useless and so is your faith. More than that, we are then found to be false witnesses about God, for we have testified about God that he raised Christ from the dead. But he did not raise him if in fact the dead are not raised. For if the dead are not raised, then Christ has not been raised either. And if Christ has not been raised, your faith is futile; you are still in your sins. Then those also who have fallen asleep in Christ are lost. If only for this life we have hope in Christ, we are to be pitied more than all men.
>
> But Christ has indeed been raised from the dead, the firstfruits of those who have fallen asleep. For since death came through a man, the resurrection of the dead comes also through a man. For as in Adam all die, so in Christ all will be made alive. But each in his own turn: Christ, the firstfruits; then, when he comes, those who belong to him. Then the end will come, when he hands over the kingdom to God the Father after he has destroyed all dominion,

authority and power. For he must reign until he has put all his enemies under his feet. The last enemy to be destroyed is death. For he "has put everything under his feet." Now when it says that "everything" has been put under him, it is clear that this does not include God himself, who put everything under Christ. When he has done this, then the Son himself will be made subject to him who put everything under him, so that God may be all in all.

Now if there is no resurrection, what will those do who are baptized for the dead? If the dead are not raised at all, why are people baptized for them? And as for us, why do we endanger ourselves every hour? I die every day—I mean that, brothers—just as surely as I glory over you in Christ Jesus our Lord. If I fought wild beasts in Ephesus for merely human reasons, what have I gained? If the dead are not raised, "Let us eat and drink, for tomorrow we die." Do not be misled: "Bad company corrupts good character." Come back to your senses as you ought, and stop sinning; for there are some who are ignorant of God—I say this to your shame.

But someone may ask, "How are the dead raised? With what kind of body will they come?" How foolish! What you sow does not come to life unless it dies. When you sow, you do not plant the body that will be, but just a seed, perhaps of wheat or of something else. But God gives it a body as he has determined, and to each kind of seed he gives its own body. All flesh is not the same: Men have one kind of flesh, animals have another, birds another and fish another. There are also heavenly bodies and there are earthly bodies; but the splendor of the heavenly bodies is one kind, and the splendor of the earthly bodies is another. The sun has one kind of splendor, the moon another and the stars another; and star differs from star in splendor.

So will it be with the resurrection of the dead. The body that is sown perishable, it is raised imperishable; it is sown in dishonor, it is raised in glory; it is sown in weakness, it is raised in power; it is sown a natural body, it is raised a spiritual body.

If there is a natural body, there is also a spiritual body. So it is written: "The first man Adam became a living being"; the last Adam, a life-giving spirit. The spiritual did not come first, but the natural, and after that the spiritual. The first man was of the dust of the earth, the second man from heaven. As was the earthly man, so are those who are of the earth; and as is the man from heaven, so also are those who are of heaven. And just as we have borne the likeness of the earthly man, so shall we bear the likeness of the man from heaven.

I declare to you, brothers, that flesh and blood cannot inherit the kingdom of God, nor does the perishable inherit the imperishable. Listen, I tell you a mystery: We will not all sleep, but we will all be changed—in a flash, in the twinkling of an eye, at the last trumpet. For the trumpet will sound, the dead will be raised imperishable, and we will be changed. For the perishable must clothe itself with the imperishable, and the mortal with immortality. When the perishable has been clothed with the imperishable, and the mortal with immortality, then the saying that is written will come true: "Death has been swallowed up in victory." (Verses 12–54)

Paul explains further in I Thessalonians 4:13–18:

> Brothers, we do not want you to be ignorant about those who fall asleep, or to grieve like the rest of men, who have no hope. We believe that Jesus died and rose again and so we believe that God will bring with Jesus those who have fallen asleep in him. According to the Lord's own word, we tell you that we who are still alive, who are left till the coming of the Lord, will certainly not precede those who have fallen asleep. For the Lord himself will come down from heaven, with a loud command, with the voice of the archangel and with the trumpet call of God, and the dead in Christ will rise first. After that, we who are still alive and are left will be caught up together with them in the clouds to meet the Lord in the air. And so we will be with the Lord forever. Therefore encourage each other with these words.

The Bible clearly teaches that when we die we "sleep" in the grave awaiting the resurrection. Some people misunderstand one of the parables of Jesus Christ, thinking it proves people go to heaven after they die. I'm talking about the parable of the Rich Man and Lazarus found in Luke 16:19–31. But is this what is really being taught in the parable? Let's read it to see what is being said.

> There was a rich man who was dressed in purple and fine linen and lived in luxury every day. At his gate was laid a beggar named Lazarus, covered with sores and longing to eat what fell from the rich man's table. Even the dogs came and licked his sores.
>
> The time came when the beggar died and the angels carried him to Abraham's side. The rich man also died and was buried. In hell [*hades*], where he was in torment, he looked up and saw Abraham far away, with Lazarus by his side. So he called to him, "Father Abraham, have pity on me and send Lazarus to dip the tip of his finger in water and cool my tongue, because I am in agony in this fire."
>
> But Abraham replied, "Son, remember that in your lifetime you received your good things, while Lazarus received bad things, but now he is comforted here and you are in agony. And besides all this, between us and you a great chasm has been fixed, so that those who want to go from here to you cannot, nor can anyone cross over from there to us."
>
> He answered, "Then I beg you, father, send Lazarus to my father's house, for I have five brothers. Let him warn them, so that they will not also come to this place of torment."

Abraham replied, "They have Moses and the Prophets; let them listen to them."

"No, father Abraham," he said, "but if someone from the dead goes to them, they will repent."

He said to him, "If they do not listen to Moses and the Prophets, they will not be convinced even if someone rises from the dead."

What is the point Jesus is making with this parable? After reading it closely, you can see there are several reasons why this parable has nothing to do with what happens to people after they die. The parable's focus is on the audience to whom Christ is speaking. Why isn't it about going to heaven or hell? First, and most importantly, God is nowhere mentioned in this parable. Why? Because the Pharisees, who were part of the audience (verse 14), put such emphasis on the law, Abraham, and Moses, they decreased the importance of God, the very one who was speaking to them through the parable. Second, if the parable was an accurate depiction of life, we would have to draw the conclusion that you go to heaven simply based on the possessions and position you have in this life: If you have a lot in this life, you go to the place of torment, and if you have little in this life, you go to be with Abraham. Belief in God and your behavior would play no role in the final judgment. If you believe this, your belief is contrary to what Christ taught while He was here on earth. Third, the Greek word used for "hell" is *hades*, not *ghehennah*, which makes a huge difference between what the Bible says happens after you die and what some people think happens. In the New Testament, the Greek words translated as "hell" are *hades*, meaning the grave, and *ghehennah*. *Ghehennah* refers to a valley where rubbish was burned outside Jerusalem and, figuratively, a place of final judgment. Right now, according to the scriptures we have read, all who have died are in "*hades*"—in the grave sleeping, awaiting resurrection.

The point of the parable is clear when the rich man tells Abraham that his brothers will repent if someone comes back from the dead and warns them. Abraham tells the rich man that if his brothers didn't listen to Moses and the Prophets, they wouldn't listen to someone who came back from the dead. This, of course, turns out to be true—Jesus Christ was resurrected from the dead and people still didn't believe or repent. The brothers most likely represent the Pharisees who, after Christ rose from the dead, paid people to deny the resurrection ever occurred. The parable wasn't about what happens to people after they die; it was to show the audience they put more stock in the law and Moses than in God. They forgot the law points to God and isn't an end in itself: worshiping *God* is the way to eternal life. Jesus Christ is the beginning and end, and the whole law points to him. So the parable is given to teach that those who lean on the law and Abraham aren't listening to what the law and Abraham taught, and they wouldn't listen to Jesus Christ, even when they witnessed His resurrection from the dead.

So the Bible teaches that those who die are "asleep" in the earth. Then they awake in a resurrection—"some to everlasting life, others to shame and everlasting contempt." The awakening of multitudes who are dead is also discussed in Revelation 20:4–6 by the apostle John: "I saw thrones on which were seated those who had been given authority to judge. And I saw the souls of those who had been beheaded because of their testimony for Jesus and because of the word of God. They had not worshiped the beast or his image and had not received his mark on their foreheads or their hands. They came to life and reigned with Christ a thousand years. (The rest of the dead did not come to life until the thousand years were ended.) This is the first resurrection. Blessed and holy are those who have part in the first resurrection. The second death has no power over them, but they will be priests of God and of Christ and will reign with him for a thousand years." Those whom God seals with His Spirit are in the first resurrection; they will be priests and kings and will not experience the second death. The second death spoken of is a final death from which there is no hope of resurrection—It's an eternal death. Because those who are in this resurrection will not experience a second death, Daniel 12:2 must be talking about another resurrection. This second resurrection is mentioned in Revelation 20:5: "(The rest of the dead did not come to life until the thousand years were ended.)" In Daniel 12:2, it says some are resurrected to everlasting life and others to shame and everlasting contempt. This is the same set of events chronicled in Revelation 20:11–15:

> Then I saw a great white throne and him who was seated on it. Earth and sky fled from his presence, and there was no place for them. And I saw the dead, great and small, standing before the throne, and books were opened. Another book was opened, which is the book of life. The dead were judged according to what they had done as recorded in the books. The sea gave up the dead that were in it, and death and Hades gave up the dead that were in them, and each person was judged according to what he had done. Then death and Hades were thrown into the lake of fire. The lake of fire is the second death. If anyone's name was not found written in the book of life, he was thrown into the lake of fire.

The lake of fire is not a place where people are tormented eternally; if that were the case, everyone would have eternal life. God says that when people are thrown into the lake of fire they experience "the second death." Since we understand the first death is the absence of life, it is the same for the second death. The second death is different from the first death because of one major point: There is no hope of resurrection from the second death. The second death is final, and the lake of fire is a place where any memory of those who are thrown into it will be completely burned and gone forever. Jesus Christ spoke about this same fire in the book of Matthew 13:37–43 in the parable of the weeds:

> He answered, "The one who sowed the good seed is the Son of Man. The field is the world, and the good seed stands for the sons of the kingdom. The weeds are the sons of the evil one, and the enemy who sows them is the devil. The harvest is the end of the age, and the harvesters are angels. As the weeds are pulled up and burned in the fire, so it will be at the end of the age. The Son of Man will send out his angels, and they will weed out of his kingdom everything that causes sin and all who do evil. They will throw them into the fiery furnace, where there will be weeping and gnashing of teeth. Then the righteous will shine like the sun in the kingdom of their Father. He who has ears, let him hear.

The last part of this verse is similar to Daniel 12:3: "Those who are wise will shine like the brightness of the heavens, and those who lead many to righteousness, like the stars for ever and ever."

We see an example of the use of "ghehennah fire," or a place of final judgment, in Matthew 10:27, 28 where Christ says to his twelve disciples: "What I tell you in the dark, speak in the daylight; what is whispered in your ear, proclaim from the roofs. Do not be afraid of those who kill the body but cannot kill the soul. Rather, be afraid of the One who can destroy both soul and body in hell." Of course "the One" being referred to in this passage is God—He has power over death—and the destruction of hell is the ghehennah fire that results in the second death from which there is no resurrection. There are several other passages in which Christ speaks about being thrown into the "hell" fire, the second death where both the body and spirit are destroyed. There are so many man-made concepts about what happens after death, but the Bible is clear on what God is going to do in the days to come. God didn't come up with this plan at the last minute or as a last resort because His other plans didn't work out. He knew at the beginning that man would sin, that Israel would turn to other gods, and that He would have to send His Son to die—that's why the symbolism of the Passover lamb was put into place back in Egypt 1,500 years before the real Passover Lamb was sacrificed at Golgotha. God did this to demonstrate His patience and love for us, that

He would go to incredible lengths, including sacrificing His only Son, to give human beings the opportunity for the ultimate gift: eternal life with Him.

After the man dressed in linen tells Daniel about the hope of resurrection, there is a description of what "those who are wise" will be doing, referring back to Daniel 11:33. These "wise" ones are people who believe and teach the truth of God. They will instruct many about true worship of the true God and about events at the end time. They will be in the first resurrection and will serve as kings and priests with Christ in the kingdom of God. This is the whole reason for Daniel Chapters 10 and 11. Remember back in verse 14 of Chapter 10 the man dressed in linen said: "Now I will tell you what will happen to your people in the future, for the vision concerns a time yet to come." The "wise will shine like the brightness of the heavens, and those who lead many to righteousness, like the stars forever and ever." This is what happens to Daniel's people in the future—It's the end result.

After the end has been revealed to Daniel, the man dressed in linen says something that isn't usually said to a prophet who has just been given a revelation:

> But you, Daniel, close up and seal the words of the scroll until the time of the end. Many will go here and there to increase knowledge. (Daniel 12:4)

Although Daniel could close up and seal the scroll at the time of his writing, he couldn't open it up at the time of the end because he wouldn't be around. What does this mean? The words of Daniel have been available since at least 200 BC, so they haven't been closed up or inaccessible to those who want to read about his experiences. The One who closes and seals the scroll is God by closing the minds of people. When he wants the words understood, He gives understanding and wisdom to the people He chooses. Things that seem so obvious to some cannot be seen by others if God chooses to keep them hidden. Take, for example, the parable of the sower talked about in Luke 8:9, 10. "His disciples asked him what this parable meant. He said, 'The knowledge of the secrets of the kingdom of God has been given to you, but to others I speak in parables, so that, "though seeing, they may not see; though hearing, they may not understand."'" It is amazing to think that when Christ was on earth, only those whose minds were opened by God could see and understand what was really happening, and even they didn't fully understand the events they were witnessing until well after they happened. But when God gave his Spirit on the day of Pentecost (another one of God's holy days mentioned in Leviticus 23), many were able to see, know, and understand. In John 14:15, Christ says to His disciples, "If you love me, you will obey what I command. And I will ask the Father, and he will give you another Counselor to be with you forever—the Spirit of truth. The world cannot accept him, because it neither sees him nor knows him. But you know him, for he lives with you and will be in you." Christ is talking about Himself—He will live with them, and He will be in them as the Spirit—because God is One. In verse 25 of the same chapter, Christ continues, "All this I have spoken while still with you. But the Counselor, the Holy Spirit, whom the Father will send in my name, will teach you all things and will remind you of everything I have said to you." Nothing has changed since that time: the Spirit is still the One who teaches and reminds those whom God is calling.

So God told Daniel the words of the prophecy would be closed until the time of the end. That means that as we approach these days, God will reveal the true meaning of the contents of the book of Daniel: all the governments of Chapters 2, 7, and 8, and who they really are; the connections those governments have had with the ancient pantheon of Zoroaster, also known as *"MYSTERY BABYLON THE GREAT THE MOTHER OF PROSTITUTES AND OF THE ABOMINA- TIONS OF THE E*ARTH" in Revelation 17:5; the events that lead to setting up the abomination that causes desolation; and a fairly good picture of the end-time "little horn" that has a mouth that speaks boastful words; the persecution of the saints; and the resurrection of the dead in Christ. All of this will be revealed in the last days by the wise who "will instruct many."

This brings us to the end of Daniel 12:4 where it says, "Many will go here and there to increase knowledge." For many years, I have heard people interpret this verse to mean people will be traveling and information will be increasing, as seen by the technological advancements of today. In other words, they believe it's a description of what our society will look like at the time of the end. It's true that because of computers and the Internet, information is increasing at a significant rate, and because of the advancement of aviation, going here and there has never been easier. However, that is not what this passage means. God is telling Daniel that what he has recorded will be sealed up until the time of the end when God will reveal the writings to people, and they, God's people, "will go here and there to increase knowledge"—the knowledge of God and what He revealed to Daniel. God is assuring Daniel that even though His words are sealed up, they will be revealed at the appointed time. The "many" mentioned in this passage are the wise, or the called-out ones, His saints, who will testify on behalf of the One Eternal God.

Then Daniel witnesses something only one other person has seen.

> Then I, Daniel, looked, and there before me stood two others, one on this bank of the river and one on the opposite bank. One of them said to the man clothed in linen, who was above the waters of the river, "How long will it be before these astonishing things are fulfilled?"
>
> The man clothed in linen, who was above the waters of the river, lifted his right hand and his left hand toward heaven, and I heard him swear by him who lives forever, saying, "It will be for a time, times and half a time. When the power of the holy people has been finally broken, all these things will be completed."

First, let's look at who these two are who join the "man dressed in linen" and who are standing on either bank of the Tigris River. No other information is given about them in the surrounding verses, but there is an account in the book of Genesis of a similar trio. In Chapter 18 verses 1 and 2, we read: "The Lord appeared to Abraham near the great trees of Mamre while he was sitting at the entrance to his tent in the heat of the day. Abraham looked up and saw three men standing nearby. When he saw them, he hurried from the entrance of his tent to meet them and bowed low to the ground." After Abraham hurried to provide food for the visitors, "The men turned away and went toward Sodom, but Abraham remained standing before the Lord" (verse 22). We find out that the two "men" were really angels: "The two angels arrived at Sodom in the evening ..." (Genesis 19:1). And the Lord, of course, was God as we see in Genesis 18:17: "Then the Lord said, 'Shall I hide from Abraham what I am about to do? Abraham will surely become a great and powerful nation, and all nations on earth will be blessed through him. For I have chosen him ...'" So here are God and two angels visiting Abraham. In the book of Daniel, two angels are called by name—Michael and Gabriel. Most likely, the two who appear before Daniel on the banks of the Tigris River are Michael, the great prince of Daniel's people, and Gabriel, the great herald who appeared earlier to Daniel (and hundreds of years later to Elizabeth and Mary to announce the births of John the Baptist and Jesus Christ). So, like Abraham, Daniel is standing before God and two great angels.

One of the angels asked God, "How long will it be before these astonishing things are fulfilled?" He is given the answer, "It will be for a time, times and half a time. When the power of the holy people has been finally broken, all these things will be completed." Usually, when the Bible speaks of "times," it means a year. But the question here is, three and a half years from what point in time? The answer is given in verse 7, and it's clearer when you flip the two sentences around: *When the power of the holy people has been finally broken, all these things will be completed. It will be for a time, times and half a time.*

All of this information was very confusing to Daniel. In Chapter 12 verse 8, he says,

> I heard, but I did not understand. So I asked, "My lord, what will the outcome of all of this be?"
>
> God said, "Go your way, Daniel, because the words are closed up and sealed until the time of the end. Many will be purified, made spotless and refined, but the wicked will continue to be wicked. None of the wicked will understand, but those who are wise will understand" (Daniel 12:9, 10).

So at the time the prophecy was given, it was closed to everyone—even the person through whom it was given! But God said that at the time of the end, "those who are wise" would understand what was happening because they'd understand the prophecy.

This last verse says so much! First, it says that God will reveal the message of this book in the last days. He was the One who sealed the words, and He will be the One who reveals the meaning of them to those He chooses. In Daniel, they are called "the wise," and in the New Testament, Christ calls them "the elect." In Matthew 24:21–25, it says, "For then there will be great distress, unequaled from the beginning of the world until now—and never to be equaled again. If those days had not been cut short, no one would survive, but for the sake of the elect those days will be shortened. At that time if anyone says to you, 'Look, here is the Christ!' or, 'There he is!' do not believe it. For false Christs and false prophets will appear and perform great signs and miracles to deceive even the elect—if that were possible. See, I have told you ahead of time." God says the elect won't be deceived about whom to follow.

Second, this verse gives the assurance that "Many will be purified"—not a small group, but *many*, and that's good news. Verse 10 also says the wicked will continue to be wicked because they won't understand. In Matthew 24:36–39, Jesus Christ says, "No one knows about that day or hour, not even the angels in heaven, nor the Son, but only the Father. As it was in the days of Noah, so it will be at the coming of the Son of Man. For in the days before the flood, people were eating and drinking, marrying and giving in marriage, up to the day Noah entered the ark; and they knew nothing about what would happen until the flood came and took them all away. That is how it will be at the coming of the Son of Man." They continued living the way they lived because they didn't understand.

Finally, the man dressed in linen leaves Daniel a short timeline of events. However, the timeline isn't for Daniel to understand, but for the wise so they'll know what will happen at the time of the end:

From the time that the daily sacrifice is abolished and the abomination that causes desolation is set up, there will be 1,290 days. Blessed is the one who waits for and reaches the end of the 1,335 days. (Daniel 12:11, 12)

We have already read in Daniel two other references to periods of time at the end of the age:

He [a king] will speak against the Most High and oppress his saints and try to change the set times and laws. The saints will be handed over to him for a time, times and half a time. But the court will sit, and his power will be taken away and completely destroyed forever. Then the sovereignty, power and greatness of the kingdoms under the whole heaven will be handed over to the saints, the people of the Most High. His kingdom will be an everlasting kingdom, and all rulers will worship and obey him. (7:25–27)

Then I heard a holy one speaking, and another holy one said to him, "How long will it take for the vision to be fulfilled—the vision concerning the daily sacrifice, the rebellion that causes desolation, and the surrender of the sanctuary and of the host that will be trampled underfoot?"
    He said to me, "It will take 2,300 evenings and mornings; then the sanctuary will be reconsecrated." (8:13, 14)

So the three end-time periods referred to are:

1. 1,290 days from the time the abomination that causes desolation is set up; blessed is the one who reaches the 1,335 days

2. 3.5 years when the saints are handed over to the stern-faced king

3. 2,300 evenings/mornings—days—until the vision is fulfilled

These verses are prophesying about the same period of time just before the arrival of Jesus Christ. What do they refer to? Let's see what we already know and what we can cautiously speculate.

Let's look at the biggest period of time first. Daniel 8:14 states it will take 2,300 evenings and mornings for the vision to be fulfilled "the vision concerning the daily sacrifice, the rebellion that causes desolation, and the surrender of the sanctuary and of the host that will be trampled underfoot." When the Bible refers to "evenings and mornings" here, it's referring to 2,300 days. When the Israelites were under the law, they were required to perform a daily sacrifice every evening and morning—"evening and morning" was considered one day. We also see in Genesis Chapter 1 the repeating verse, "And there was evening, and there was morning—the first [second, third, etc.] day." So it appears this 2,300-day time period—or around six and a half years—involves the entire reign of the little horn, most likely including the time leading up to his ascension to power until the return of Jesus Christ. Take a look at the earlier verses in Chapter 8:9–12:

> Out of one of them came another horn, which started small but grew in power to the south and to the east and toward the Beautiful Land. It grew until it reached the host of the heavens, and it threw some of the starry host down to the earth and trampled on them. It set itself up to be as great as the Prince of the host; it took away the daily sacrifice from him, and the place of his sanctuary was brought low. Because of rebellion, the host of the saints and the daily sacrifice were given over to it. It prospered in everything it did, and truth was thrown to the ground.

I believe this passage describes events that will occur over this 2,300-day time period.

As we discussed earlier, the abolishment of the daily sacrifice near the end of the age describes a time when the saints are handed over to be persecuted, as we read in Daniel 8:11, 12. We know that the Anointed One, Jesus Christ, put an end to sacrifice once and for all: God no longer requires the laws and sacrificial system of the old covenant. God has no plan to reinstitute a morning and evening animal sacrifice on Mount Moriah; in fact, if something is set up there in the future, you can be sure it is not from God! This is the place where "the abomination that causes desolation" will be set up, though we don't know exactly what it will look like. It's possible that this "abomination" will look like something good to most people, but the Bible says they will be deceived. God's people, "the wise," will know this event is a sign that the time of the end is well underway.

I believe within this period of 2,300 days are the "1,290 days" and "1,335 days" Daniel is told about. What do these shorter periods of time refer to? Scripture tells us, "From the time that the daily sacrifice is abolished and the abomination that causes desolation is set up, there will be 1,290 days." God has a plan that He is following. Mankind doesn't know the exact days, but He says "at the appointed time" what He has prophesied will occur. We can get into slippery territory trying to pinpoint exact dates, but the scriptures tell us that well into the 2,300-day period the sanctuary will be surrendered and the host (saints) will be trampled underfoot, given over to the little horn. But what is meant by the verse, "Blessed is the one who waits for and reaches the end of the 1,335 days"? What is happening to the saints during these forty-five days?

Rapture?

"Blessed is the one who waits for and reaches the end of the 1,335 days." That's all it says: no explanation. So we'll have to go to other books in the Bible to see if we can understand what the forty-five days might refer to. (This is based on the assumption that the 1,335 days don't start *before* the 1,290 days; if that were the case, they would both end at the same time.) Addressing these forty-five days means we also need to address a topic that piques the interest of many Christians—the rapture. The rapture is usually defined as the time when those called by God will be swept up into heaven to be spared the awful events that will take place on earth just before Jesus Christ returns. But as we've read in Chapters 8 and 11 of Daniel, instead of a rapture, the people called by God have been warned of persecution and death. But there *will* be a time when the people who worship God will be swept up to be with Him. In Matthew 24, Jesus Christ describes the events preceding His return:

> Immediately after the distress of those days "the sun will be darkened, and the moon will not give its light; the stars will fall from the sky, and the heavenly bodies will be shaken." At that time the sign of the Son of Man will appear in the sky, and all the nations of the earth will mourn. They will see the Son of Man coming on the clouds of the sky, with power and great glory. And he will send his angels with a loud trumpet call, and they will gather his elect from the four winds, from one end of the heavens to the other." (Verses 29–31)

There is more information in I Thessalonians 4:13–18:

> Brothers, we do not want you to be ignorant about those who fall asleep, or to grieve like the rest of men, who have no hope. We believe that Jesus died and rose again and so we believe that God will bring with Jesus those who have fallen asleep. For the Lord himself will come down from heaven, with a loud command, with the voice of the archangel and with the trumpet call of God, and the dead in Christ will rise first. After that, we who are still alive and are left will be caught up together with them in the clouds to meet the Lord in the air. And so we will be with the Lord forever. Therefore encourage each other with these words."

The power of the holy people will be broken for three and a half years when truth and knowledge of God will be thrown to the ground and trampled, and then the saints will finally rise to heaven in a cloud. Then what? The answer is found in Revelation 19:5–9:

"Praise our God, all you his servants, you who fear him, both small and great!"

Then I heard what sounded like a great multitude, like the roar of rushing waters and like loud peals of thunder, shouting:

"Hallelujah! For our Lord God Almighty reigns. Let us rejoice and be glad and give him glory! For the wedding of the Lamb has come, and his bride has made herself ready. Fine linen, bright and clean, was given her to wear." (Fine linen stands for the righteous acts of the saints.)

Then the angel said to me, "Write: 'Blessed are those who are invited to the wedding supper of the Lamb!'" And he added, "These are the true words of God."

I believe the additional forty-five days Daniel is told about are after the 1,290 days and they involve one of the most incredible events of all time: the wedding supper of the Lamb—Jesus Christ—and His bride the church. All people who worship God will be at the greatest wedding feast ever held. Just think of the people who will be there: Abraham and Sarah, Kings David and Solomon, all of the prophets, the apostles, and all the people God has ever called! It's an event too great for the human mind to fully appreciate. Of course, the One who will absolutely be there is the bridegroom—Jesus Christ. Can you imagine walking amongst the guests at this incredible event? The attire for this wedding is "fine linen, bright and clean"—symbolically the "righteous acts of the saints." Later, in verse 14 of Revelation 19, it says the armies of heaven will be wearing "fine linen, white and clean." This is also what the messenger is wearing—"a man dressed in linen"—as He speaks to Daniel.

Jesus Christ often used the symbolism of wedding and marriage to teach. His first recorded miracle was changing six jars of water into probably the finest wine ever to touch the lips of man at the wedding feast at Cana.

On the third day a wedding took place at Cana in Galilee. Jesus' mother was there, and Jesus and his disciples had also been invited to the wedding. When the wine was gone, Jesus' mother said to him, "They have no more wine."

"Dear woman, why do you involve me?" Jesus replied. "My time has not yet come."

His mother said to the servants, "Do whatever he tells you."

Nearby stood six stone water jars, the kind used by the Jews for ceremonial washing, each holding from twenty to thirty gallons.

Jesus said to the servants, "Fill the jars with water"; so they filled them to the brim. The he told them, "Now draw some out and take it to the master of the banquet."

They did so, and the master of the banquet tasted the water that had been turned into wine. He did not realize where it had come from, though the servants who had drawn the water knew. Then he called the bridegroom aside and said, "Everyone brings out the choice wine first and then the cheaper wine after the guests have had too much to drink; but you have saved the best till now." (John 2:1–11)

Think of how good that wine must have tasted—wine made by God! I include this story here because it symbolizes all of what God has done and will do: save the best for last. The Master and the Bridegroom will hold a wedding feast at the end of the age because He has saved the best till the end.

Another place in the New Testament where a wedding is mentioned is Matthew 22:1–14.

Jesus spoke to them again in parables, saying: "The kingdom of heaven is like a king who prepared a wedding banquet for his son. He sent his servants to those who had been invited to the banquet to tell them to come, but they refused to come.

"Then he sent some more servants and said, 'Tell those who have been invited that I have prepared my dinner: My oxen and fatted cattle have been butchered, and everything is ready. Come to the wedding banquet.'

"But they paid no attention and went off—one to his field, another to his business. The rest seized his servants, mistreated them and killed them. The king was enraged. He sent his army and destroyed those murderers and burned their city.

"Then he said to his servants, 'The wedding banquet is ready, but those I invited did not deserve to come. Go to the street corners and invite to the banquet anyone you find.' So the servants went out into the streets and gathered all the people they could find, both good and bad, and the wedding hall was filled with guests.

"But when the king came in to see the guests, he noticed a man there who was not wearing wedding clothes. 'Friend,' he asked, 'how did you get in here without wedding clothes?' The man was speechless.

"Then the king told the attendants, 'Tie him hand and foot, and throw him outside, into the darkness, where there will be weeping and gnashing of teeth.'

"For many are invited, but few are chosen."

This parable encapsulates the whole history of God's relationship with Israel. The king is the Father who sent His only Son to die for sin; the Son is the bridegroom; and the wedding occurs at the end of the age when the saints are gathered from the four winds of the earth. The servants are the prophets, and the invited people are the nation of Israel. After they refused to pay any attention to God and mistreated and killed His prophets, God destroyed Israel and burned Jerusalem.

Then, God the King sent his prophets to invite not only the people of Israel, but also the people who are not of the promise, the Gentiles. The Father wants those who are interested in attending the wedding of His Son, and He has put out an invitation to those He would like to have in attendance. There are wedding clothes given to all the guests. Even though the type of clothing isn't mentioned in this parable, we know what the garments are—fine white linen. But who is the one who is without wedding clothes? Interestingly, he represents the point of the whole parable. The audience Jesus Christ is talking to is mentioned two verses back in Matthew 21:45, 46: "When the chief priests and the Pharisees heard Jesus' parables, they knew he was talking about them. They looked for a way to arrest him, but they were afraid of the crowd because the people held that he was a prophet."

And in verse 43 of Chapter 21, Jesus says, "Therefore I tell you that the kingdom of God will be taken away from you and given to a people who will produce its fruit." The man without wedding clothes decided to show up at the wedding, but simply being there wasn't enough: he needed clothes of fine linen—the righteous acts of the saints.

Another parable about a wedding is given in Matthew 25:1–13. This time, the warning is to be ready for the wedding, even though the bridegroom may appear to be late in arriving.

"At that time the kingdom of heaven will be like ten virgins who took their lamps and went out to meet the bridegroom. Five of them were foolish and five were wise. The foolish ones took their lamps but did not take any oil with them. The wise, however, took oil in jars along with their lamps. The bridegroom was a long time in coming, and they all became drowsy and fell asleep.

"At midnight the cry rang out: 'Here's the bridegroom! Come out to meet him!'

"Then all the virgins woke up and trimmed their lamps. The foolish ones said to the wise, 'Give us some of your oil; our lamps are going out.'

"'No,' they replied, 'there may not be enough for both us and you. Instead, go to those who sell oil and buy some for yourselves.'

"But while they were on their way to buy the oil, the bridegroom arrived. The virgins who were ready went in with him to the wedding banquet. And the door was shut.

"Later the others also came. 'Sir! Sir!' they said. 'Open the door for us!'

"But he replied, 'I tell you the truth, I don't know you.'

"Therefore keep watch, because you do not know the day or the hour."

The message of this parable is be patient and ready because the bridegroom is coming and the wedding *will* take place!

All of these stories and parables of weddings are symbolic of the church as the bride being prepared for Jesus Christ, the bridegroom, and the wedding that will take place after He gathers His elect from all over the earth. After the wedding supper, the Bridegroom and His bride will return to earth to set up the kingdom of God, the very kingdom mentioned in Daniel 2:44 and 7:14. And it is my belief that this wedding will take place at the end of the 1,290 days and the wedding feast will conclude at the end of the 1,335 days.

Now for the final verse of this incredible book, the book of Daniel: "As for you, go your way till the end. You will rest, and then at the end of the days you will rise to receive your allotted inheritance." This last message to Daniel from the man dressed in linen, the Word of God, contains three critical points. First, God had finished His work with Daniel as a prophet; the work for him was complete. Second, Daniel was to live out the rest of his days, and then at the appointed time, he would die. God, however, used the term "rest" instead of death, just like He did in John 11:11, because it is a rest, or sleep, that all will be awakened from. "Some to everlasting life, others to shame and everlasting contempt."

In Luke 20:34–38, we see the certainty of the resurrection. Jesus gives an answer to those trying to trick him with a problem involving the resurrection. "The people of this age marry and are given in marriage. But those who are considered worthy of taking part in that age and in the resurrection from the dead will neither marry nor be given in marriage, and they can no longer die; for they are like the angels. They are God's children, since they are children of the resurrection. But in the account of the bush, even Moses showed that the dead rise, for he calls the Lord 'the God of Abraham, and the God of Isaac, and the God of Jacob.' He is not the God of the dead, but of the living, for to him all are alive."

This same Jesus says in Revelation 2:17, 18, "Do not be afraid. I am the First and the Last. I am the Living One; I was dead, and behold I am alive for ever and ever! And I hold the keys of death and Hades." How encouraging that God holds the keys to death and He will unlock the grave so all may be resurrected to life. Satan, the one who deceived us into choosing death, has been defeated by the Anointed One who came "to finish transgression, to put an end to sin, to atone for wickedness, to bring in everlasting righteousness" so that all may have life again because our God is the God of the living.

And third, Daniel is given the greatest news any human could ever receive: He will be resurrected in the first resurrection and will be given an inheritance from

God in His kingdom. Daniel will be at the wedding supper when the King of kings will be among His officials, the elect. For Daniel, it will almost be like old times when he served the greatest kings of the earth; however, this time he will be serving the Living God in the greatest kingdom the earth will ever know, and that kingdom, unlike those in Daniel's time, will never end.

A Message to the Elect "in the Time of Those Kings"

"At that time the Son of Man will appear in the sky, and all the nations of the earth will mourn. They will see the Son of Man coming on the clouds of the sky, with power and great glory. And he will send his angels with a loud trumpet call, and they will gather his elect from the four winds, from one end of the heavens to the other."
Matthew 24:30-31

Daniel 2:44 says, "In the time of those kings, the God of heaven will set up a kingdom that will never be destroyed, nor will it be left to another people. It will crush all those kingdoms and bring them to an end, but it will itself endure forever." After reading this book, some might ask, "What if all that is written here comes to pass? What if we are in the time of the end? What do we do now?"

The answer is given by Jesus Christ in Matthew 24:42, "Therefore keep watch, because you do not know on what day your Lord will come." What do we watch for? There are three important areas to watch for in what we believe is the time of wrath (Daniel 8:19).

First—watch yourself. God tells us to look at ourselves, not our neighbors. There is no admonition found in scripture against judging yourself. A good measuring rod is found in Matthew Chapters 5, 6, and 7; judging yourself using the words of Jesus Christ means there's enough work to last a lifetime! After Peter was filled with the Holy Spirit and spoke to the crowd of people about what God had done for them by sacrificing His Son, they asked:

> "Brothers, what shall we do?"
> Peter replied, "Repent and be baptized, every one of you, in the name of Jesus Christ for the forgiveness of your sins. And you will receive the gift of the Holy Spirit. The promise is for you and your children and for all who are far off—for all whom the Lord our God will call."

To repent means to be sorry for what you've done and to ask forgiveness from God, because it's against Him that we sin—sin is disobeying God. Romans 6:23 says, "For the wages of sin is death, but the gift of God is eternal life in Christ Jesus our Lord." When we sin—disobey God—we incur the penalty of death, but Jesus Christ died for us. Because of this, we can be forgiven, and then the Father and the Son can live in us through the Holy Spirit, allowing God's mind in us. "Each of you should look not only to your own interests, but also to the interests of others. Your attitude should be the same as that of Christ Jesus: Who, being in very nature God, did not consider equality with God something to be grasped, but made himself nothing, taking the very nature of a servant, being made in human likeness. And being found in appearance as a man, he humbled himself and became obedient to death—even death on a cross!" (Philippians 2:4–8). Our attitude is to be the same as Christ's—taking on the nature of a servant, being humble, and being obedient to God even if it means death. Shadrach, Meshach, and Abednego understood that. With the Holy Spirit in you, Galatians 5:16–25 says:

> So I say, live by the Spirit, and you will not gratify the desires of the sinful nature. For the sinful nature desires what is contrary to the Spirit, and the Spirit what is contrary to the sinful nature. They are in conflict with each other, so that you do not do what you want. But if you are led by the Spirit, you are not under law.
>
> The acts of the sinful nature are obvious: sexual immorality, impurity and debauchery; idolatry and witchcraft; hatred, discord, jealousy, fits of rage, selfish ambition, dissensions, factions and envy; drunkenness, orgies, and the like. I warn you, as I did before, that those who live like this will not inherit the kingdom of God.
>
> But the fruit of the Spirit is love, joy, peace, patience, kindness, goodness, faithfulness, gentleness and self-control. Against such things there is no law. Those who belong to Christ Jesus have crucified the sinful nature with its passions and desires. Since we live by the Spirit, let us keep in step with the Spirit.

Be merciful and forgiving just as our Father in heaven is incredibly merciful and forgiving toward us. And pray always; keep in contact with our Father who is always available to listen to our thanksgivings and concerns. If you have requests of God, remember the words of Jesus Christ in Matthew 7:7–12,

> Ask and it will be given to you; seek and you will find; knock and the door will be opened to you. For everyone who asks receives; he who seeks finds; and to him who knocks, the door will be opened. Which of you, if his son asks for

bread, will give him a stone? Or if he asks for a fish, will give him a snake? If you, then, though you are evil, know how to give good gifts to your children, how much more will your Father in heaven give good gifts to those who ask him! So in everything, do to others what you would have them do to you, for this sums up the Law and the Prophets.

Remember that Christianity is not a political movement. If it was, Christ would have admonished Caesar when He was here on earth. He didn't; in fact, He said, "Give to Caesar what is Caesar's, and to God what is God's." The elect's citizenship is with the coming kingdom of God, and it is there that our efforts and hope should rest. We should, when given an opportunity, talk about what God will do when His Son will set up the kingdom of God here on earth. However, people often try to set up the kingdom through man's existing governments. The scriptures are quite clear that it is Jesus Christ coming down from heaven with power, majesty, and glory that will usher in the beginning of His kingdom, not a candidate winning an election from a particular political party, or the spreading of democracy throughout the world. We should also keep in mind that we cannot legislate people's moral behavior. One of the most interesting passages found in scripture is Revelation 22:10, 11: "Then he told me, 'Do not seal up the words of the prophecy of this book, because the time is near. Let him who does wrong continue to do wrong; let him who is vile continue to be vile; let him who does right continue to do right; and let him who is holy continue to be holy.'" So many well-intentioned people try to change the behavior of others, but few quote from this passage. Should we preach the good news and be examples of godly living? Yes, but we should be mindful of this passage when talking to others. Not everyone will understand. A variation of this same passage is also found in Daniel 12: "Go your way, Daniel, because the words are closed up and sealed until the time of the end. Many will be purified, made spotless and refined, but the wicked will continue to be wicked. None of the wicked will understand. But those who are wise will understand."

The main thing to remember is what Christ said in Matthew 7:1–6:

> "Do not judge, or you too will be judged. For in the same way you judge others, you will be judged, and with the measure you use, it will be measured to you. Why do you look at the speck of sawdust in your brother's eye and pay no attention to the plank in your own eye? How can you say to your brother, 'Let me take the speck out of your eye,' when all the time there is a plank in your own eye? You hypocrite, first take the plank out of your own eye, and then you will see clearly to remove the speck from your brother's eye."

So we are to watch ourselves, obeying God by doing what He says to do: worshiping Him and loving others as ourselves.

Second—watch what and how you worship. God describes Himself as a jealous God, and after reading Chapter 5 in this book regarding true worship of the true God, we realize that God takes worship very seriously. *He* has prescribed how we should worship Him, and the only way He's pleased by worship is if we worship Him like He has told us to. If we choose to worship Him in our own way, we are disobeying Him—sinning—so it's worth going over what is true worship and what isn't. Let's take a look at some of things God said He wanted.

God wants us to worship only Him in spirit and truth, and He tells us clearly that He is *one* God. Moses tells Israel, "These are the commands, decrees and laws the Lord your God directed me to teach you to observe in the land that you are crossing the Jordan to possess, so that you, your children and their children after them may fear the Lord your God as long as you live by keeping all his decrees and commands that I give you, and so that you may enjoy long life … Hear, O Israel: The Lord our God, the Lord is one. Love the Lord your God with all your heart and with all your soul and with all your strength" (Deuteronomy 6:1–5). Again, this is repeated in the New Testament when Jesus is asked what the most important commandment is. "'The most important one,' answered Jesus, 'is this: "Hear O Israel, the Lord our God, the Lord is one. Love the Lord your God with all your heart and with all your soul and with all your mind and with all your strength."'"

While many religions worship several gods, or one great god with other minor gods, or one god who's actually three gods, God says He is one God and we are to worship only Him. The Father, Jesus Christ, and the Holy Spirit are not three in one, they are one. Jesus Christ said in John 10:27–30, "My sheep listen to my voice; I know them, and they follow me. I give them eternal life, and they shall never perish; no one can snatch them out of my hand. My Father, who has given them to me, is greater than all; no one can snatch them out of my Father's hand. I and the Father are one."

God also says, "You shall have no other gods before me. You shall not make for yourself an idol in the form of anything in heaven above or on the earth beneath or in the waters below. You shall not bow down to them or worship them; for I, the Lord your God, am a jealous God, punishing the children for the sin of the fathers to the third and fourth generation of those who hate me, but showing love to a thousand generations of those who love me and keep my commandments" (Exodus 5:7–10). God states clearly that we are to worship only

Him and that we aren't to have anything as an idol or something to be worshiped.

Almost all religions still have statues and symbols included in their worship and that includes the most famous symbol of them all—the cross. Many Christians may not know that the cross is an ancient pagan symbol that goes back at least to the Egyptians, well before the time of Christ's crucifixion. The history of the cross can easily be researched in a good encyclopedia, and even a brief look through a concordance shows there is no reference in the Bible to crosses being used in worship. Since the apostles were Jewish, they would have been very wary of idols, and we should have that same attitude. When we worship God, we need to remember that Christ died *and* was resurrected; there is no need to constantly keep the instrument of His death hanging on the walls or the top of church buildings, as jewelry around our necks, on Bibles, or on T-shirts, etc., as we worship Him.

Just as we should be careful not to worship idols or symbols, we should also be careful of the traditions we use to worship God. As this book covered earlier, many Christian traditions originated from ancient pagan worship traditions. The days of Christmas, Halloween, Easter, Palm Sunday, Good Friday, and Lent are not found as holy days in the Bible, and a quick look into the history of these days reveals they were originally used to worship gods other than the true God. Taking days used to worship other gods and putting new symbolism to them doesn't please God; it is impossible to use these days to worship God.

What about God? Does He have any days or seasons? The short answer is yes. The days God commanded Israel to keep under the old covenant are listed in Leviticus 23: "The Lord said to Moses, 'Speak to the Israelites and say to them: "These are my appointed feasts, the appointed feasts of the Lord, which you are to proclaim as sacred assemblies."'" These days are: the Sabbath, Passover, Wave Sheaf Offering, Feast of Unleavened Bread, Pentecost, Feast of Trumpets, Atonement, Feast of Tabernacles, and the Last Great Day. All of these days are part of what is known as the law, the law given to Moses at Sinai (the other parts of the law are ritual sacrifices and offerings). These are the only days listed in the Bible as days God commanded for worship. These feasts are still kept by many Jewish people and Christians who believe the old covenant (law) is still in effect. If people wanted to, they could still celebrate these days. These days and seasons point to Christ in what He has done or will do. For example, Jesus Christ, the Lamb of God, died on Passover at exactly the same time the lambs were to be slaughtered in commemoration of Israel's salvation from Egypt. Hence, Jesus Christ is the Passover, and He died so that Israel, and all humans, could have salvation from death. Jesus Christ fulfilled the Passover, and it's that event that gives us the opportunity for salvation: resurrection from death and the blessing of being with God for eternity. Furthermore, the apostle Paul frequently mentioned that the Gentiles did not need to keep the law although many of the Jewish Christians kept it (all new covenant church members were Jewish for many years, and they kept the law until Peter welcomed Cornelius, the first Gentile, at Caesarea in Acts 10), but the Gentile members of the church were not bound to keep the Law of Moses; they were bound to the new law which was faith in the saving grace of Jesus Christ. Paul explains this issue in many of his letters to the churches, but I think he expresses it best in the book of Galatians 4:21–31 and 5:1–6. In Galatia, many Jewish Christians were teaching that one had to keep the law to be saved, but Paul said that the law could not save, only faith in Christ.

> Tell me, you who want to be under the law, are you not aware of what the law says? For it is written that Abraham had two sons, one by the slave woman and the other by the free woman. His son by the slave woman was born in the ordinary way; but his son by the free woman was born as a result of a promise.
>
> These things may be taken figuratively, for the women represent two covenants. One covenant is from Mount Sinai and bears children who are to be slaves: This is Hagar. Now Hagar stands for Mount Sinai in Arabia and corresponds to the present city of Jerusalem, because she is in slavery with her children. But the Jerusalem that is above is free, and she is our mother. For it is written:
>
> "Be glad, O barren woman, who bears no children; break forth and cry aloud, you who have no labor pains; because more are the children of the desolate woman than of her who has a husband." [This quote is from Isaiah 54:1.]
>
> Now you, brothers, like Isaac, are the children of the promise. At that time the son born in the ordinary way persecuted the son born by the power of the Spirit. It is the same now. But what does the Scripture say? "Get rid of the slave woman and her son, for the slave woman's son will never share in the inheritance with the free woman's son." Therefore, brothers, we are not children of the slave woman, but of the free woman.
>
> It is for freedom that Christ has set us free. Stand firm, then, and do not let yourselves be burdened again by a yoke of slavery.
>
> Mark my words! I, Paul, tell you that if you let yourselves be circumcised, Christ will be no value to you at all. Again I declare to every man who lets himself be circumcised that he is obligated to obey the whole law. You who are trying to be justified by law have been alienated from Christ; you have fallen away from grace. But by faith we eagerly await through the Spirit the righteousness for which we hope. For in Christ Jesus neither circumcision nor

uncircumcision has any value. The only thing that counts is faith expressing itself through love.

I don't think there is a more condemning passage in the Bible than what is written here in Galatians. Paul says continuing to be under the law is continuing in slavery. So what was the reason for the law? Paul explains in Galatians 3:15–29 why God gave the law to Israel:

> Brothers, let me take an example from everyday life. Just as no one can set aside or add to a human covenant that has been duly established, so it is in this case. The promises were spoken to Abraham and his seed. The Scripture does not say "and to his seeds," meaning many people, but "and to your seed," meaning one person, who is Christ. What I mean is this: The law, introduced 430 years later, does not set aside the covenant previously established by God and thus do away with the promise. For if the inheritance depends on the law, then it no longer depends on a promise; but God in his grace gave it to Abraham through a promise.
>
> What, then, was the purpose of the law? It was added because of transgressions until the Seed to whom the promise referred had come. The law was put into effect through angels by a mediator. A mediator, however, does not represent just one party; but God is one.
>
> Is the law, therefore, opposed to the promises of God? Absolutely not! For if a law had been given that could impart life, then righteousness would certainly have come by the law. But the Scripture declares that the whole world is a prisoner of sin, so that what was promised, being given through faith in Jesus Christ, might be given to those who believe.
>
> Before this faith came, we were held prisoner by the law, locked up until faith should be revealed. So the law was put in charge to lead us to Christ that we might be justified by faith. Now that faith has come, we are no longer under the supervision of the law.
>
> You are all sons of God through faith in Christ Jesus, for all of you who were baptized into Christ have clothed yourselves with Christ. There is neither Jew nor Greek, slave nor free, male nor female, for you are all one in Christ Jesus. If you belong to Christ, then you are Abraham's seed, and heirs according to the promise.

The law was given until Christ came and gave Himself as a sacrifice, allowing repentance from sin. How very interesting that we are deep into the New Testament and Paul is talking about Abraham. Paul says that if you have faith and are baptized into Christ, then you are an heir to the promise made to Abraham back in Genesis 15 and 22. Earlier in this book, we said that one of the most important events in the Bible is when God swears by Himself that He will bless all nations through Abraham's seed: "The angel of the Lord called to Abraham from heaven a second time and said, 'I swear by myself, declares the Lord, that because you have done this and have not withheld your son, your only son, I will surely bless you and make your descendants as numerous as the stars in the sky and as the sand on the seashore. Your descendants will take possession of the cities of their enemies, **and through your offspring [seed] all nations on earth will be blessed,** because you have obeyed me'" (Genesis 22:15–18). All the activities that are recorded in the Bible are linked to that very promise God Himself made.

So true worship is important to God. John 4:23, 24 says: "Yet a time is coming and has now come when the true worshipers will worship the Father in spirit and truth, for they are the kind of worshipers the Father seeks. God is spirit, and his worshipers must worship in spirit and in truth."

Third—watch world events. "Remember the former things, those of long ago; I am God, and there is no other; I am God, and there is none like me. I make known the end from the beginning, from ancient times, what is still to come. I say: My purpose will stand, and I will do all that I please" (Isaiah 46:9, 10). God gives us prophecy in the Bible for a reason, but, contrary to what many people believe, it's not for the purpose of pinpointing the "end of the world." Through prophecy, God reveals how great He is; He knows the end from the beginning because He has set His plan in motion, and mankind and Satan can't derail it. Prophecy is also used by God to encourage those who worship and believe Him. We're reminded that even though everything seems upside down and backwards, God has a plan and it's unfolding the way He has determined. In the book of Daniel, God tells us about the kingdoms that will rule until He finally destroys them and sets up His eternal kingdom. God uses the end-time prophecies in Daniel to encourage His people through very tough times. He also gives us prophecy so we can recognize what's going on. Reading through Daniel, we learned there will be a leading power of the Christian West—most likely the United States of America—that will begin to wane and lose its influential role, followed by a conglomeration of Western Christian nations that fill the vacuum of power. Islamic power in the Middle East, probably led by Iran, will continue to clash with Western Christianity. China and the counties of East Asia will become actively involved in the Middle East, which will eventually lead to the major world powers and their armies amassing there for battle.

Matthew 24:23–25 tells us there will be an increase in false teachings, and it will seem so true that we're told even those who worship the true God would be deceived **"if that were possible."** Be familiar with what the Bible says will happen and check it against everything you hear. The biblical books of Matthew,

Mark, and Luke report what Christ said regarding how He will return: "At that time the sign of the Son of Man will appear in the sky, and all the nations of the earth will mourn. They will see the Son of Man coming on the clouds of the sky, with power and great glory." Any other teaching is not in concert with the Word of God, and therefore misleading and false. Watch for persecution of those who follow Christ—Christ and the book of Daniel forecast a severe persecution before His return: "Then you will be handed over to be persecuted and put to death, and you will be hated by all nations because of me. At that time many will turn away from the faith and will betray and hate each other, and many false prophets will appear and deceive many people" (Matthew 24:9–11). When you see this, you'll know that the time of the end is very near. Watch for the eventual rise in a strong religious/nationalistic power that many will feel is the solution to the world's problems. That power will be the one that is the persecutor of those that follow the Lamb of God. When all this occurs, don't be alarmed or surprised—all of this is supposed to happen.

Finally, watch Jerusalem and, more specifically, Mount Moriah, the very place where the religious power will set up false worship. Jesus Christ said,

> "So when you see standing in the holy place 'the abomination that causes desolation,' spoken of through the prophet Daniel—let the reader understand—then those who are Judea flee to the mountains. Let no one on the roof of his house go down to take anything out of the house. Let no one in the field go back to get his cloak. How dreadful it will be in those days for pregnant women and nursing mothers! Pray that your flight will not take place in winter or on the Sabbath. For then there will be great distress, unequalled from the beginning of the world until now—and never to be equaled again. If those days had not been cut short, no one would survive, but for the sake of the elect those days will be shortened. At that time if anyone says to you, 'Look here is the Christ!' or, 'There he is!' do not believe it. For false Christs and false prophets will appear and perform great signs and miracles to deceive even the elect—if that were possible. See, I have told you ahead of time." (Matthew 24:15–25)

◆   ◆   ◆

God gives prophecy for a reason, and that reason isn't so we can pinpoint the day of Christ's return. Instead, the prophecies in the book of Daniel are given so that those who know God and worship Him will know He has a plan and He is carrying it out. He has given power to certain kingdoms, building them up and bringing them down, and at the appointed time, He will destroy the final kingdoms and set up His everlasting kingdom. Even though everything may seem upside down to those who worship Him, we can be comforted that this is all in God's hands.

And finally, in Revelation 22, we read about the fulfillment of the blessing of all nations that God promised would be given through Abraham's seed, Jesus Christ:

> Then the angel showed me the water of life, as clear as crystal, flowing from the throne of God and of the Lamb down the middle of the great street of the city. On each side of the river stood the tree of life, bearing twelve crops of fruit, yielding its fruit every month. And the leaves of the tree are for the healing of the nations. No longer will there be any curse. The throne of God and the Lamb will be in the city, and his servants will serve him. They will see his face, and his name will be on their foreheads. There will be no more night. They will not need the light of a lamp or the light of the sun, for the Lord God will give them light. And they will reign for ever and ever.

"I heard, but I did not understand. So I asked, 'My lord, what will the outcome of all this be?'

"He replied, 'Go your way, Daniel, because the words are closed up and sealed until the time of the end. Many will be purified, made spotless and refined, but the wicked will continue to be wicked. None of the wicked will understand, but those who are wise will understand.'"

Daniel 12:8–10

Endnotes

1. C. F. Pfeiffer, "Israel, History of the People of," *The International Standard Bible Encyclopedia.* Vol. 2, pp. 908–924 (1979).

2. S. J. Schultz, "Jehoiakim," *The International Standard Bible Encyclopedia.* Vol. 2, pp. 976–977 (1979).

3. R. E. Hayden, "Persia," *The International Standard Bible Encyclopedia.* Vol. 3, pp. 776–780 (1979).

4. I. S. Bible Encyclopedia vol. 2, p. 266.

5. W. S. Lasor, "Jerusalem," *The International Standard Bible Encyclopedia.* Vol. 2, pp. 998–1032 (1979).

6. R. E. Hayden, "Persia," *The International Standard Bible Encyclopedia.* Vol. 3, pp. 776–780 (1979).

7. "Alexander the Great," *The Funk and Wagnalls New Encyclopedia.* Vol. 1, pp. 368–370 (1986).

8. J. E. H. Thomson, "Alexander the Great," *The International Standard Bible Encyclopedia.* Vol. 1, pp. 87–89 (1979).

9. "Cleopatra," *The Funk and Wagnalls New Encyclopedia.* Vol. 6, pp. 359–360 (1986).

978-0-595-48595-6
0-595-48595-2

Printed in Great Britain
by Amazon.co.uk, Ltd.,
Marston Gate.